John Ball's
In the Heat of the Night

Adapted by Matt Pelfrey

A SAMUEL FRENCH ACTING EDITION

SAMUEL FRENCH
FOUNDED 1830

NEW YORK HOLLYWOOD LONDON TORONTO

SAMUELFRENCH.COM

ISBN 978-0-573-69892-7   Printed in U.S.A.   #29695

MUSIC USE NOTE

JOHN BALL'S IN THE HEAT OF THE NIGHT was first produced by God-light Theatre Company at 59E59 Theaters March 19-April 25, 2010. The production was directed by Joe Tantalo, with production design by Maruti Evans, sound design by Elizabeth Rhodes, costume design by Virginia Monte, choreography by Hachi Yu, and fight choreography by Rick Sordelet. The production stage managers were Christina Hurtado, Meredith Brown, and Derek Shore. The cast was as follows:

NOREEN PURDY	Scarlett Thiele
SAM WOOD	Nick Paglino
CHIEF GILLESPIE	Gregory Konow
PETE	Lawrence Jansen
CHARLES TATUM/ENDICOTT/AL JENNINGS	Adam Kee
CORONER/MAYOR SCHUBERT/KLANSMAN	Michael Shimkin
VIRGIL TIBBS	Sean Phillips
HARVEY OBERST/PURDY/KLANSMAN	Ryan O'Callaghan
MELANIE TATUM	Julianne Nelson
ERIC KAUFMAN/RALPH/KLANSMAN	Bryce Hodgson

CHARACTERS

Actor #1: Chief Gillespie

Actor #2: Virgil Tibbs

Actor #3: Sam Wood

Actor #4: Pete/Man In Shadows/Klansman 1

Actor #5: Harvey Oberst/Purdy/Klansman

Actor #6: Charles Tatum/Endicott/Al Jennings

Actor #7: Coroner/Mayor Schubert/Klansman

Actor #8: Eric Kaufman/Ralph/Klansman

Actor #9: Melanie Tatum

Actor #10: Noreen Purdy

- When double or triple casting, many other configurations are possible. This is how the premier production devided up the roles.
- Barfly 1 &2 were not used in the original production.

Scene One

(Night.
Sticky and hot.
A radio plays...songs...a bit of news perhaps...We're in
Argo, Alabama...it's 1962.
Someone sits in a dark car.
Face barely visible in the glow of a cigarette.
It's just him. And the dark. And the heat. And the red
glow of the cigarette.
His name is **SAM WOOD**, *late 20s, and he's a police officer.*
SAM *just sits there.*
For the longest time.
Not moving.
But suddenly –
He stiffens. Sits up. Stubs out his cigarette.
He sees what he's been waiting for...
Hoping for...
In a window, she appears.
Her name is **NOREEN PURDY**. *From the looks of her, she*
could be anywhere from sixteen to twenty one.
No matter what her age is, she's stunning.
She has a raw, reckless sexuality to her.
Her hair slick with sweat.
Shirt unbuttoned.
She uses the unbuttoned shirt like wings, flapping them
to cool her perspiring body.
After a long moment, she peels her shirt off. Uses it to dry
her forehead.
Her neck.
Between her breasts.
She lingers at the window for a moment, then steps
away...
She's gone.

SAM *bites his lip, disappointed.*
But then...
NOREEN *steps back to the window.*
Holds an ice cold glass of lemonade.
She takes a long, cool drink.
Now she seems to be looking right at Sam.
SAM *slides down in his seat.*
A long moment, then...
She pulls the blind.
Lights fade.)

Scene Two

(Darkness.
A fan whirs.
Night bugs chirp.
4 A.M.
Hot.
Moonlight through a window.
A phone rings in the dark.
Someone groans, then –
A light turns on.
GILLESPIE *sits up in bed. Grabs the phone.)*

GILLESPIE. *(groggy)* Gillespie…

PETE. Chief…

GILLESPIE. Yeah…?

PETE. …hate to wake you –

GILLESPIE. Who is this?

PETE. Pete. Chief, its P –

GILLESPIE. What is it?

PETE. We got us a problem.

GILLESPIE. Talk.

PETE. Yeah, it's pretty late –

GILLESPIE. Goddammit, get to it!

PETE. Well, if Sam's right, we may have a first-class murder on our hands.

(That gives him a jolt –)

GILLESPIE. Wait – what?

PETE. We got us a murder! Sam –

GILLESPIE. Sam's dead?

PETE. No – Sam found a body! A murdered body, sir.

(He's waking up a bit more now.)

GILLESPIE. You shittin' me?

PETE. No, sir.

GILLESPIE. Who?

PETE. Don't know.

GILLESPIE. Local?

PETE. Not sure yet.

GILLESPIE. Where – ?

PETE Will Keith Rd, Chief, just below Johnson.

(long pause)

Whatcha' want me to do?

(GILLESPIE *has to think about that a moment. Then –)*

GILLESPIE. Nothin'. Don't do anything. I'm on my way.

(He stands up. Takes a big breath, then very slowly lets it out…)

(Lights shift to:)

Scene Three

(The road.
Police lights drench the stage.
A body sprawled on the ground. GILLESPIE, SAM
WOOD.)

GILLESPIE. Where's the wallet?

SAM WOOD. Didn't find it, Chief.

GILLESPIE. Not on the body?

SAM WOOD. No, sir.

GILLESPIE. You look?

SAM WOOD. That's Charles Tatum.

GILLESPIE. Not what I asked.

SAM WOOD. Sorry. I looked around. Nothing.

   (beat)

GILLESPIE. Charles Tatum…

SAM WOOD. Real estate guy…

GILLESPIE. I know who Tatum is.

SAM WOOD. Sorry.

   *(**GILLESPIE** runs a hand through his hair, staring at the*
   body, scans the area –)

GILLESPIE. How long's he been dead?

SAM WOOD. Hour or less? Who done this can't be far.

GILLESPIE. All I asked was how long he's been dead.

SAM WOOD. Sorry.

GILLESPIE. I know my goddamn job. You think I don't, we
   can have that talk.

SAM WOOD. Yes, sir. Sorry –

GILLESPIE. And stop sayin' sorry. "Sorry, sorry, sorry" every
   five seconds. You're like a goddamn mosquito in my
   ear.

SAM WOOD. Sorry, si –

(**GILLESPIE** *looks around, perhaps we get the impression he's buying time, thinking about exactly what he's supposed to do here. Finally...*)

GILLESPIE. Chalk 'im, then get me pictures from all angles. And keep traffic away – throw up a barricade or something.

SAM WOOD. Yes sir.

GILLESPIE. Take your car, check the railroad station and the north end of town, see if anyone's crazy enough to try hitchhiking outta here.

(**SAM** *stands there, waiting to see if there are more instructions coming.*)

Get going for chrissake.

SAM WOOD. Yes, sir – sorry – I mean –

GILLESPIE. Go!

(**SAM** *scuttles off.*)

(*staring at the body*) Son-of-a-bitch...

(*Lights shift to:*)

Scene Four

(The Train Station.
A dim light reveals an **AFRICAN AMERICAN MAN**
*[***TIBBS***], well dressed, waiting for a train.*
SAM *enters cautiously, sees the* **AFRICAN AMERICAN**
MAN.
He visually reacts, shocked to actually see someone.
Retreating around the corner, he takes a moment to
compose himself as –
Lights change.
For a moment, the Train Station Vanishes.
Only **SAM**'*s face is visible in a shaft of light. Then…*
In another place and time
CHARLES TATUM, *50, appears.*
Alive.
It's night. **TATUM** *walks down the street.*
The **AFRICAN AMERICAN MAN** *materializes from the*
darkness. He pulls a crowbar from inside his jacket.
TATUM *checks his watch. Stops. Looks around, as if lost.*
The **AFRICAN AMERICAN MAN** *creeps up from the*
shadows and –
SLAM! Cracks him over his head.
TATUM *drops…tries to cover himself. The* **AFRICAN**
AMERICAN MAN *continues hitting* **TATUM**, *but in the*
scuffle he loses his grip on the crowbar and finishes
TATUM *by strangling him with his bare hands.*
It's brutal and sad and pathetic.
Now with his victim dead, The **AFRICAN AMERICAN**
MAN *rifles through Tatum's pockets, steals his wallet*
and vanishes.
Lights widen on **SAM**. *He takes a breath and pulls his*
gun.
Lights return to normal.
The **AFRICAN AMERICAN MAN** *as he was, sitting on the*
bench.
SAM *slips from cover, slinks up to The* **AFRICAN AMER-**
ICAN MAN *and –)*

SAM WOOD. On your feet, black boy. Now! On your fucking feet!

(The **AFRICAN AMERICAN MAN** *reaches for his coat.)*

No you don't. Don't! Hands where I can see 'em.

*(***SAM** *grabs him, slams him face first into the wall.)*

Fingers apart and lean against 'em. Don't move 'til I say, understand?

*(***SAM** *takes the man's wallet. Full of cash.* **SAM** *excited. Pats him for a weapon.)*

You're commin' with me. One false move, I drop you with a bullet in your spine. Got me? No quick moves.

*(***SAM** *gets his radio.)*

Wood from the railroad station. Bringing in a colored suspect. I repeat, I got me a colored suspect!

(He hangs up.)

You stepped in shit this time boy. You stepped in a big ol' pile a shit.

(Lights shift to:)

Scene Five

(Police Station. Gillespie's office.
GILLESPIE *faces The* **AFRICAN AMERICAN SUSPECT**
[TIBBS].
SAM *stands nearby.)*

GILLESPIE. You know your name, boy?

(beat)

Hm?

(beat)

You know your name, don'tcha?

(beat)

I'm waitin', goddamnit.

SAM WOOD. Answer the Chief, boy...

(long pause)

TIBBS. I know my name.

GILLESPIE. Know what kind a trouble you're in?

TIBBS. Why don't you tell me.

GILLESPIE. Sam, this boy got attitude?

SAM WOOD. Seems that way.

GILLESPIE. We're off to a bad start.

SAM WOOD. Chief don't like a bad start.

GILLESPIE. Shut up, Sam.

SAM WOOD. Sorry. I mean, I'm...

(But **GILLESPIE** *ignores Sam, focused on his prisoner –)*

GILLESPIE. Don't like it this hot. Just hangs on you. Makes people smell like animals when you can't wipe the sweat away fast enough. Heat like this, don't matter how many showers you take. Two minutes later you're sticky again. Reminds us what we really are, deep down. Same with killin'. Fact is, I got just about everything I hate right here in this goddamn room. An' it's got me itchy. Itchy an' pissed off. Now tell me your goddamn name!

TIBBS. Virgil Tibbs.

GILLESPIE. What you in such a rush to leave for, Virgil Tibbs?

TIBBS. Was I in a rush?

GILLESPIE. What're you doin' in my station?

TIBBS. Waiting for the train.

GILLESPIE. Which one?

TIBBS. Five-seventeen.

SAM WOOD. That's to Montgomery?

TIBBS. Correct.

GILLESPIE. When an' how'd you get here?

TIBBS. Local…from downstate.

GILLESPIE. Keep goin'. What's downstate?

TIBBS. My mother.

GILLESPIE. Just a good boy visiting Mommy?

(*TIBBS doesn't answer.*)

She give you all this money? She a rich old lady? She reach into her mattress and give it to ya?

TIBBS. Earned it.

GILLESPIE. Boy like you can't earn money like this.

TIBBS. You bet I did.

GILLESPIE. Don't play it like this, boy. At least come up with a better story –

TIBBS. Every penny.

GILLESPIE. Think I'm stupid?

TIBBS. Not yet.

GILLESPIE. Oh, you're beggin' for a thrashin', boy.

TIBBS. Just answering the questions bein' asked.

GILLESPIE. Even if you could make this kind of scratch, you'd spend it faster than a hummingbird fucks. You people don't know how to hold your money. Get paid, you act like it's the first time you seen a dollar bill.

(*TIBBS doesn't take Gillespie's bait.*)

GILLESPIE. *(cont.)* So where's it you work, makes you this money? Maybe I just live in the wrong part'a the country.

TIBBS. California.

GILLESPIE. Where in California?

TIBBS. Pasadena.

(beat)

Near Los Angeles.

GILLESPIE. I know where the hell it is!

(beat)

Find a pot a gold out there in queersville?

(no answer)

What is it you do, boy?

TIBBS. I'm a police officer.

(beat)

GILLESPIE. Hope you're not expectin' me to believe that?

TIBBS. I don't expect anything from you.

(A long moment. Finally, **GILLESPIE** *pulls* **SAM** *aside.)*

GILLESPIE. You question this man any before you brought him in?

SAM WOOD. No, sir.

GILLESPIE. Why the fuck not?

SAM WOOD. Your orders were check the railroad station, then look –

GILLESPIE. Alright, alright, shut up...

*(***GILLESPIE*** *moves back to* **TIBBS***.)*

You're a cop in California?

TIBBS. There's an ID in my wallet.

*(***GILLESPIE*** *picks up the wallet with the air of handling something distasteful and unclean.*

He looks at Tibb's ID.)

GILLESPIE. You know we wouldn't let the likes of you be a cop down here, don'tcha?

(beat)

That was a question.

TIBBS. You assume I'd wanna be a cop here.

(beat)

Now, if it's all the same, the sooner I get back the better.

GILLESPIE. You're not going anywhere. Not until I say so. Not until I check up on you. Sam, get 'im outta here. Throw 'im in detention.

(to **TIBBS***)*

And pardon my lack'a manners, boy: Welcome to Argo, Alabama.

(Lights shift to:)

Scene Six

(Restroom.
A sign says 'MEN - WHITE.'
SAM *splashes his face.*
PETE, *a police officer who works the night desk, takes a leak.)*

PETE. Whooooeee! I'm tellin' you, Sam, old big shot Gillespie's gonna take this one right in the cornhole!

SAM WOOD. Keep your goddamn voice down!

PETE. He ain't gonna hear.

SAM WOOD. Pete, I'm serious. I like my job and I need my job!

PETE. Fine, fine…

*(***PETE*** *shuts up, smiling, finishes pissing.* **SAM** *dries his face with a towel.)*

(beat)

SAM WOOD. So what you got?

PETE. Oh, now you wanna hear what I gotta say?

SAM WOOD. Just don't scream it at the top'a yer lungs.

PETE. Gillespie sent a wire to Pasadena sniffin' up on the black boy you caught.

SAM WOOD. Don't blame him.

PETE. Shit, of course not. By the looks, I wouldn't be surprised he ain't one of those agitators set on causin' trouble.

(beat)

So wait 'till you hear what we got back. "Confirm Virgil Tibbs, member Pasadena Police Department, past five years. Before that, member of the Los Angeles Police department."

SAM WOOD. I'll be damned.

PETE. Gets better.

SAM WOOD. Doubt that.

PETE. Present rank, Investigator. Reputation: excellent. Specialist: homicide.

SAM WOOD. Ho-lee-shit!

PETE. And here's the goddamn kicker: Sons a bitches out there in California say: Advise if his services are needed. Can you believe that? "Advise if services are needed!"

(**PETE** *cackles.*)

SAM WOOD. Wow.

PETE. Bet you next month's pay Gillespie don't know a damn thing about 'vestigatin' no homicide. Don't know how he got this job in the first place.

SAM WOOD. We'll see.

PETE. Don't tell me you like 'im? Practically treats you like a nigger.

SAM WOOD. He treats me like he treats everyone else. Like he treats you. Don't start shit with me.

PETE. He's full of 'imself. Prolly figures this'll set him up for something bigger down the road.

SAM WOOD. How'd you get all this dope?

PETE. I find out what I wanna find out.

(**SAM** *moves to go.*)

PETE. And I tell ya, if I get a chance to see Gillespie twist in the wind, this'll be good no matter how it goes down.

SAM WOOD. What's got you so worked up on the Chief?

PETE. Ain't you noticed? The man is a first rate asshole and a world-class sonuvabitch.

SAM WOOD. A boss a' mine bein' an asshole ain't new to me. But I guess you've lived a privileged life up to now.

PETE. Plus, it ain't right they made him Chief. He ain't from around here. Job belonged to Cliff Longers.

SAM WOOD. 'Cept he was a white knight.

PETE. So what? You got a problem with The Boys?

(SAM shrugs.)

Far as I'm concerned they should just let them Klan boys be the law, you'd see this state runnin' like a top. We sure as shit wouldn't be having these niggers thinkin' they own the place. Or worse: nigger-lovin' jews comin' in with their bus rides and sit-ins an whatnot.

SAM WOOD. Maybe you're right. I dunno…

PETE. Course I'm right, Sam. You know I am. This whole damn country's goin' in the wrong direction. Got them faggot Kennedy boys runnin' their mouths off and niggers thinkin' they know somethin'. This Tatum fella ain't gonna be the only body layin' in the street if this shit don't get taken care of soon.

SAM WOOD. What's Tatum have to do with that?

PETE. I heard they was plannin' on cartin' in black boys to do all the building they got planned.

SAM WOOD. You'll believe anything, won't ya, Pete.

PETE. Can't stick your head in the sand, Sam. Gonna be a time to take a stand.

SAM WOOD. I gotta get back.

PETE. Yeah, you do.

(An odd moment between SAM and PETE, then:
SAM *exits.*
Lights shift to:)

Scene Seven

(Hallway. **SAM** *rushing out from the bathroom almost slams into* **GILLESPIE,** *who looks even more annoyed than usual.)*

GILLESPIE. Jesus, Sam! Watch out!

SAM WOOD. Sorry, Chief.

GILLESPIE. Lookin' for you anyway. Go see Tatum's daughter at Endicott's place. Get to her before she hears about this shit some other way. Understand?

SAM WOOD. Yes, sir. I'm on it.

*(***SAM*** *exits.* **GILLESPIE** *takes a moment, collecting himself, before heading into…)*

Scene Eight

(Detention. **GILLESPIE** *and* **TIBBS**.*)*

GILLESPIE. Pasadena says you're a hotshot.

TIBBS. Doubt those were the words.

GILLESPIE. Ever look at dead bodies?

TIBBS. More'n I'd like.

GILLESPIE. Gonna look at one now.

> *(Pause.* **GILLESPIE** *expects some kind of response, but gets nothing from* **TIBBS**.*)*

Suppose you come along.

TIBBS. No thanks.

GILLESPIE. It'll keep you out of trouble.

TIBBS. Am I in trouble?

GILLESPIE. Not yet.

TIBBS. I'll just wait for my train.

GILLESPIE. Missed it already.

TIBBS. Then the next one.

GILLESPIE. Won't be another for a long while. Let's go.

> *(***GILLESPIE*** *unlocks the cell door.)*

TIBBS. I'd rather not get in your way.

GILLESPIE. I wouldn't let ya.

TIBBS. I don't see the point. From what I've seen, you got things under control.

GILLESPIE. The point is I asked you.

TIBBS. Askin' or tellin'.

GILLESPIE. Come on, Tibbs. I seen it in your eyes this entire time.

TIBBS. Seen what?

GILLESPIE. You wanna show this dumb cracker how you earn that fat paycheck. Ain't that right, boy? You can tell me the truth. Cause I sure as shit'll be honest with you: I wanna know how you do it. I wanna see if that badge is real or just something they give away for free. You got the attitude, but other than that, I'm not sure I'd let you wash my car's windows.

(The gauntlet is thrown. A long moment, then…)

TIBBS. Let's go.

(Lights shift to:)

Scene Nine

(Morgue. **GILLESPIE**, **TIBBS**, *Tatum's body, and* **THE CORONER**.*)*

THE CORONER *bristles when he sees Tibbs.)*

CORONER. What's goin' on here, Chief?

GILLESPIE. This man works for the Pasadena Police Department.

CORONER. So what?

GILLESPIE. I'm lettin' him tag along with me. That okay with you?

CORONER. No, it ain't. But it's your call.

GILLESPIE. Damn right it is. *(to* **TIBBS***)* Well, Virgil, there you go. It's all yours.

*(***TIBBS** *goes to examine the body.*
He raises the dead man's hands, examines first the palms, then the fingernails.)

TIBBS. New manicure.

GILLESPIE. That important?

TIBBS. Maybe.

*(***GILLESPIE** *looks to* **CORONER**.
CORONER *shrugs.*
TIBBS *replaces the hand, moves up to peer at the massive head wound.)*

TIBBS. I'll need silver nitrate and acetic acid.

CORONER. *(to* **GILLESPIE***)* He talkin' to me?

TIBBS. Yes. I'm talking to you.

CORONER. We don't got any a' that shit.

*(***TIBBS** *looks at Coroner, then to Gillespie.)*

TIBBS. Ammonium hydrosulfide?

CORONER. Nope.

*(***TIBBS** *gets the picture.)*

TIBBS. Can you get some?

CORONER. S'pose I could make some calls.

TIBBS. It would be a help.

CORONER. See what I can do.

TIBBS. I'll give you a list of other items, but in the meantime, how about some tooth picks?

CORONER. Yeah, that I can rustle up. Hold on.

> (**CORONER** *exits.*
> **GILLESPIE** *watches* **TIBBS** *work.*
> **TIBBS** *rubs one hand alongside the cheek and jaw of the dead man.*
> **TIBBS** *progresses to the feet. Gently, he unties one of the dead man's shoes, places the shoe on the floor, removes one sock and examines the foot and ankle.*
> **TIBBS** *examines the knees of the dead man's trousers.*
> **CORONER** *enters and hands* **TIBBS** *the toothpicks.*)

TIBBS. Much appreciated.

> (**CORONER** *waits, interested in how they'll be used in the autopsy.*
> **TIBBS** *puts one in his mouth, the rest in his pocket.*)

CORONER. *(annoyed)* What's this about? *(to* **CHIEF***)* Who is this boy anyway?

GILLESPIE. Already told you.

> (**TIBBS** *glances at his watch.*)

TIBBS. What time was this man killed?

GILLESPIE. Wood found him, 3. A.M.

CORONER. I put time of death about an hour earlier.

TIBBS. *(to be clear)* At two?

CORONER. Maybe a little later. 2-2:15 - 2:30.

> (**TIBBS** *feels the face again.*)

TIBBS. Rigor's begun.

CORONER. No, it ain't.

TIBBS. Feel his jaw.

> (**CORONER** *does. By his look, he realizes Tibbs is right.*)

The time of death has to be earlier. We've got post-mortem lividity in the legs.

(Embarrassed, **THE CORONER** *glares at Tibbs.)*

TIBBS. *(cont.)* Can I assume you have a thermometer here?

CORONER. We do.

TIBBS. I wanna check the loss of heat from the brain. It's the best way to determine time of death.

(beat)

Ain't that right Chief?

GILLESPIE. Always been my favorite method, Tibbs.

*(***PETE*** *races in –)*

PETE. Chief! It's Harvey Oberst – He's runnin' like a Jack Rabbit!

GILLESPIE. What – ?

PETE. It's Oberst –

GILLESPIE. Speak so I can understand you goddammit!

PETE. I'm sorry – He's runnin'! They got him cornered in the old mill. He tried to make a run for it but –

GILLESPIE. That dumb piece a' white trash… *(to* **TIBBS***)* Don't you go nowhere!

*(***GILLESPIE*** *flies out the door.* **PETE** *follows.)*

*(***CORONER** *stares at* **TIBBS***. He clearly doesn't like being alone with him. Over this –)*

(Sound of hunting dogs barking.
Heavy breathing – like a man running, tearing through bushes, grunting as he falls, etc.
Then shouts: a fight, a struggle, punches landed, grunts of pain…
Lights shift to:)

Scene Ten

(Police Station. **GILLESPIE** *slams through the front door –)*

GILLESPIE. Damn, did that squirrely prick put a fight! I'll give 'im that. The boy can run, but he can't outrun the hounds.

PETE. Where is he?

GILLESPIE. Andy and Mitch taking 'im around back.

(beat)

Shit, sun's barely up and we caught ourselves a murderer. How you like that?

*(**TIBBS** enters from hallway.)*

TIBBS. You got your man?

GILLESPIE. Like I said, we know our business.

TIBBS. There a confession?

GILLESPIE. Punk had Tatum's wallet.

PETE. Hot damn! Red handed! You nailed 'im, chief! You nailed 'im!

TIBBS. But no admission of guilt?

GILLESPIE. That's comin' up in just a few minutes.

TIBBS. I'd like to observe.

GILLESPIE. Watch and learn.

(Lights shift to:)

Scene Eleven

(A cramped and hot interrogation room.
OBERST *slumped in a chair. He's sweaty, and has a bloody nose.*
He's got a nervous, frightened disposition – like a roach worried about getting squashed.
TIBBS *watches near the door as* **GILLESPIE** *gets in Oberst's face.)*

GILLESPIE. You had his wallet!

OBERST. – It was just laying out there. I just –

GILLESPIE. Sure it was. Sure...

OBERST. Was walking by – so, so –

GILLESPIE. Thought you'd help yourself?

OBERST. If I didn't someone else would, so yeah, why not?

GILLESPIE. Sure, most people'd just start rootin' around a dead body –

OBERST. Ain't like that – you don't know!

GILLESPIE. I do know! You killed this man for his money. You thought, "This is the free pass I been waitin' for."

OBERST. Bullshit!

GILLESPIE. "I do this one thing and" –

OBERST. NO!

GILLESPIE. You did!

OBERST. I DIDN'T, GODDAMN YOU!

(a long beat
Then –)

GILLESPIE. Oh, yes. Yes, you did. You sure as hell did.

(Lights change:)

*(***CHARLES TATUM*** appears in another place and time. It's the night of the murder. He's walking down the street.*
OBERST *approaches* **TATUM** *as if preparing to attack him...physically he's in that reality, but he continues to talk and interact with* **GILLESPIE** *and* **TIBBS**.*)

GILLESPIE. *(cont.)* You knew he was a big shot! Real Estate guy walkin' around at night, fixin' to buy up half the city, now that's a boy who's gotta have some money on 'im, ain't that what you were thinkin'?

OBERST. No!

GILLESPIE. Big shot workin' for someone like Endicott's gotta be loaded.

OBERST. He was laying there, his –

GILLESPIE. You thought, "This man is askin' for it!"

OBERST. YOU STOP SAYIN' THAT!

> *(And with that outburst, **OBERST** attacks **TATUM**. He tries to grab **TATUM** from behind.*
> *They scuffle.*
> ***OBERST** wrestles Tatum's cane from him.*
> ***TATUM** makes a break for it.*
> ***OBERST** chases him, catches him, throws him against a wall and beats him to death.*
> *Horrified by what he's done, he backs away from the crumpled body and throws the murder weapon aside as he reenters the jail scene:)*

OBERST. *(cont.)* You got it dead wrong...DEAD WRONG –

GILLESPIE. The fuck I do!

OBERST. Man, I ain't followin' what Endicott's doin'...

GILLESPIE. Everyone knows he's got Tatum down here buyin' up property!

OBERST. Well, I don't! And I don't give a shit, either! Got plenty'a my own problems.

GILLESPIE. You sure as hell do.

OBERST. Ya don't know crap about me, Gillespie!

GILLESPIE. Here's what I know: You got a murdered man's wallet. And I'm tellin' you, kid, that is all I need.

OBERST. He couldn't use it – if not me, someone else – One'a your own men!

GILLESPIE. You're just twistin' here...

OBERST. You know what I'm talkin' about –

GILLESPIE. What'd you bash that skull in with?

OBERST. You tell me 'cause I don't know.

GILLESPIE. A rock? You sprayed that man's brains all over the street!

OBERST. He was a little guy, I could've handled him easy if I'd wanted to! All I did – I'm tellin' you – is pick his fuckin' wallet. Nothin' else!

GILLESPIE. *(into intercom)* Pete! Get in here!

(PETE runs in.)

PETE. Yeah, chief?

GILLESPIE. Book him. Suspicion of murder.

PETE. That'd be my pleasure. *(to OBERST)* C'mon, dipshit.

(PETE hauls OBERST out.)

(GILLESPIE turns to TIBBS.)

GILLESPIE. This how fast you catch murderers in your neck of the woods?

TIBBS. Might need to dig a little deeper.

GILLESPIE. Excuse me?

TIBBS. Don't think he's your man, Chief.

GILLESPIE. You bought that kid's story? Shit, I thought you were supposed to be the hotshot cop? *(sneers)* Maybe you should take notes for your people on the coast. Not sure how they do it out there, but I'll tell you one thing: I ain't impressed.

TIBBS. You want the results of my examinations?

GILLESPIE. I know all I need about the body.

TIBBS. You know Oberst's left handed?

GILLESPIE. So what if he is?

TIBBS. The fatal blow was with a blunt instrument.

GILLESPIE. I know.

TIBBS. And delivered at an angle of about seventeen degrees from the right and from behind. That makes it almost certain the assailant was right-handed.

GILLESPIE. Maybe he is, maybe he ain't, but –

TIBBS. When Oberst thumped himself in the chest he did it with his left hand.

GILLESPIE. That's thin, Tibbs.

TIBBS. Then there's his shoes. And the fact he needs a shave.

(**GILLESPIE** *just stares at Tibbs, refusing to ask why, not willing to concede more territory to this man.*)

Tatum was hit from behind. Means he was either assaulted by someone he knew and trusted, who stepped behind him for a moment, or, more likely, someone sneaked up quietly enough to hit him without warning. If Tatum had been warned, even by a second, he'd've turned his head and the blow would've landed at a different angle.

(*beat*)

Your suspect's wearing hard leather heels and has steel plates to make them last longer. In those shoes every step is noisy. He couldn't possibly've made a surprise attack with them on.

GILLESPIE. Have you considered a man might, oh, I don't know, CHANGE HIS FUCKING SHOES?

TIBBS. But you mentioned this man is poor white trash, which suggests he has only a limited number of shoes and doesn't change often...

(**GILLESPIE** *laughs, shakes his head.* **TIBBS** *continues, undeterred:*)

Judging by the stubble on his chin, I'd guess he was up all night. If he went home to change his shoes, he'd probably shave.

GILLESPIE. So fucking what? Maybe he didn't! I didn't shave last night!

TIBBS. But we know he does so regularly. There're razor nicks under this chin that showed that.

(**GILLESPIE**, *keeping his rage deep inside, just stares at* **TIBBS** *for a good, long moment.*)

GILLESPIE. *(sarcastic)* Pretty sure of yourself, ain'tcha, Virgil?

TIBBS. I just do the job in front of me.

(As if Gillespie doesn't?)

GILLESPIE. *(seething)* Virgil's a pretty fancy name for a black boy.

TIBBS. *(sharp)* Not really.

GILLESPIE. What do they call you where you're from?

(pause)

TIBBS. They call me Mr. Tibbs.

*(The moment hangs there. **GILLESPIE** looks like he's about to go at Tibbs when –)*

*(**SAM** enters.)*

SAM WOOD. Chief –

(He sees he's interrupted something.)

I'm sorry…

GILLESPIE. *(doesn't take his eyes from **TIBBS**)* Don't know how to knock anymore, Sam?

SAM WOOD. I'm sorr – I'm…I was at Endicotts and –

GILLESPIE. You break the news?

SAM WOOD. I did, and, uh, they asked to come down and talk to you.

GILLESPIE. They?

SAM WOOD. Endicott and Tatum's daughter…But I can have 'em wait, or…

GILLESPIE. Not necessary. Send 'em in. You ain't inter-rupted shit.

SAM WOOD. Yes, sir.

*(**SAM** motions out the door, steps aside as **MR. ENDICOTT** and Tatum's daughter, **MELANIE**, enter. Both looked haggard and grief-stricken. **MELANIE**, especially, is a wreck…)*

GILLESPIE. Mr. Endicott…

ENDICOTT. Thanks for seeing us, Chief…

GILLESPIE. I hope Sam expressed our condolences to you and Ms. Tatum.

ENDICOTT. He did. Thank you. But to brass tacks: Do we have any idea who…?

GILLESPIE. Not yet. No. But we will.

ENDICOTT. I want to help. I want to get who did this.

GILLESPIE. When Ms. Tatum feels able, we'd like to have her formally identify the body.

ENDICOTT. Can I do that?

GILLESPIE. Sir?

ENDICOTT. I don't want her to go through that.

GILLESPIE. …I'm sure that'll be fine.

ENDICOTT. *(to Melanie)* If I can spare you seeing her father like –

MELANIE. I don't want to be spared…

(She looks like she's shut down some part of herself to subdue her grief…she avoids eye contact, speaks in a low voice…like all of her energy is going into a battle to control her emotions.)

ENDICOTT. You're in no condition to…

MELANIE. What condition should I be in?

(silence)

*(stronger, to **GILLESPIE**)*

I…do not want to be spared.

GILLESPIE. Understood.

MELANIE. Who'd do something like this?

SAM WOOD. Don't know, Ma'am. But you can be damned sure we're gonna find out.

*(**GILLESPIE** glares at **SAM**. He shrinks back a little bit, but can't take his eyes off **MELANIE**.)*

ENDICOTT. I know you and your department will do everything possible to find and punish the person who did this. Whatever I can do to help, I want you to call on me. I don't care what it is. Understand?

GILLESPIE. We're gonna do our best to –

TIBBS. *(cutting in)* Can you tell us what the nature of your relationship was?

(All eyes go to **TIBBS**, *sitting in the corner.)*

*(***MELANIE*** *wipes her eyes, also looking at* **TIBBS**.*)*

ENDICOTT. Who are you?

GILLESPIE. He's a police investigator out in Los Angeles, California.

TIBBS. Pasadena.

GILLESPIE. What difference does it make?

ENDICOTT. I haven't heard your name.

GILLESPIE. Call him, "Mr. Tibbs."

(Beat. **TIBBS** *glances at* **GILLESPIE**, *then to* **ENDICOTT**:*)*

TIBBS. Virgil Tibbs.

ENDICOTT. What is it you do out there?

TIBBS. I specialize in crimes against persons – homicide, rape, and similar major offences.

MELANIE. And you're here because…?

GILLESPIE. Sam found Virgil waiting for a train and brought him in as a possible suspect. Then we found out who he was.

MELANIE. How long are you in Argo?

TIBBS. Just 'till the next train.

(It's impossible to tell what **ENDICOTT** *or* **MELANIE** *think of* **TIBBS**.*)*

MELANIE. My father is a …was…a real estate developer.

ENDICOTT. We're buying properties on the West side… Charles was helping me on a commercial project. We're putting in a department store and a movie theatre.

TIBBS. Anyone you know might not like your plans?

ENDICOTT. This could've been because of me?

TIBBS. At this point, we're just asking questions…looking for anything.

ENDICOTT. This project will provide jobs in the demolition, in the construction, and steady employment with the businesses themselves. Plus, we'll pull in traffic for every other business in Argo. Who the hell would have a problem with that? I suppose there are interests in town who oppose me...don't like me for personal or political reasons...but why any of that would be transferred to Tatum...

(beat)

Anything else at the moment? I think Ms. Tatum should rest.

MELANIE. I'm not tired.

ENDICOTT. None the less...

GILLESPIE. No. Go ahead. We'll be in touch.

TIBBS. One last thing.

ENDICOTT. Yes?

TIBBS. What kind of department store?

ENDICOTT. Woolworths.

TIBBS. Who else has been working with you and Mr. Tatum?

MELANIE. Eric.

ENDICOTT. Yes. Eric Kaufman.

TIBBS. He'll need to be interviewed.

GILLESPIE. *(an edge in his voice)* Sam, see them out.

(**ENDICOTT, MELANIE** *and* **SAM** *exit.*)

(**GILLESPIE** *explodes* –)

Let's get something straight here, Tibbs: I don't like being interrupted. An' I sure as hell don't like bein' second guessed. Not in my station and not in front of someone like Endicott. That too much for you to understand?

TIBBS. Not at all.

GILLESPIE. N'fact, This might be a good time to get yourself back to the station. No reason to risk missing another train.

TIBBS. I couldn't agree more.

(*beat*)

Good luck with your investigation. I'm sure you'll get your man in no time.

(**TIBBS** *offers his hand to shake.* **GILLESPIE** *doesn't take it. He turns away.*)

Can I get Sam to drive me to the station?

GILLESPIE. No, Tibbs, ya can't. I need all my men right where they are. Walkin' ain't gonna kill you.

(*beat*)

(**TIBBS** *exits as*)

(*Lights shift to:*)

Scene Twelve

(Police Station Lobby. **SAM** *catches up with* **TIBBS**. **PETE** *watches as he does desk work.)*

SAM WOOD. Hold on, Virgil…

TIBBS. Hmm?

SAM WOOD. …just wanted to, ah… *(notices* **PETE**, *tries to lower his voice a bit)* …just, you know, say "thanks."

TIBBS. What for?

SAM WOOD. Letting me off the hook with the false arrest thing.

TIBBS. Not the first time it's happened to me.

SAM WOOD. Still, you could've made it tough…

TIBBS. You like what you do here, Sam?

SAM WOOD. What'd'you mean?

TIBBS. Police work.

SAM WOOD. S'pose so.

(beat)

TIBBS. Been good to meet you.

*(***TIBBS** *extends his hand to shake.*
Awkward moment as **SAM** *isn't sure what to do, but then he shakes hands with* **TIBBS**.
PETE *eyes all of this.)*

Maybe I'll see you out in California some day.

*(***TIBBS** *exits.)*
*(***PETE** *stares at* **SAM**.)*

SAM WOOD. Fuck off, Pete.

*(***SAM** *exits.* **PETE** *shakes his head, disgusted with* **SAM**.)*

Scene Thirteen

(**GILLESPIE** *in his office when* **PETE** *sticks his head in.*)

PETE. You got a call.

GILLESPIE. And when I turn off the intercom, it's 'cause I don't wanna talk to nobody.

PETE. I know…but it's Mayor Schubert.

(**PETE** *exits.*)

(**GILLESPIE** *sighs, mouths "fuck."*
He takes a moment, then picks up the phone.)

GILLESPIE. Gillespie.

FRANK. This is Frank Schubert.

(*Mayor* **FRANK SCHUBERT** *appears in a separate light.*)

GILLESPIE. Yep?

FRANK. What's going on down there?

GILLESPIE. We got a murder.

FRANK. I'm talking about this colored detective your boys spaded up.

GILLESPIE. That's taken care of.

FRANK. Then why the hell'd I just get a call from Pasadena confirming a request to borrow your boy for a few days.

GILLESPIE. I didn't call nobody. An' I sure as shit don't need no help with –

FRANK. Goddamn Endicott…

GILLESPIE. What about 'im?

FRANK. He's got a boner for the black boy and he made the call. Thinks he might do some good. I assumed you were already on board for some dumb reason and thanked the son-of-a-bitch kindly.

GILLESPIE. This's the first I heard about it. Endicott's a goddamn meddler.

FRANK. Tell me something I don't know.

(*pause*)

GILLESPIE. So what is it you expectin' me to do here?

FRANK. Take care of it.

GILLESPIE. Meanin' what?

FRANK. Meanin' use the boy.

GILLESPIE. The hell I will.

FRANK. Yeah, the hell you will.

GILLESPIE. Bullshit, Frank. My station. I'm runnin' it the way I want an' I sure as shit ain't gonna let some outsider run my investigation!

FRANK. You're overlooking something here Bill.

GILLESPIE. N'what's that?

FRANK. This boy gives you the perfect out.

GILLESPIE. Who says I need one?

FRANK. Suppose this detective finds the man you want?

GILLESPIE. Suppose I find the –

FRANK. *(cutting him off)* Just shut up a damn second and listen: He ain't got no police powers here.

GILLESPIE. So what?

FRANK. So he'll have to hand the whole damn thing over to you.

GILLESPIE. And if he screws it up I eat the shit?

FRANK. Well. Then he takes the fall doesn't he? And so does Endicott. Either way, you win. But if you don't use 'im, and by some strange twist of fate you don't apprehend the killer…well, it's all on you. And you alone. And whether or not you and I find Endicott to be a cocksucker, he still has a lot a' pull in this town. And I sure as shit don't want him backing anyone else for Mayor next year, if you follow.

(pause)

GILLESPIE. I just kicked 'im out.

FRANK. Well then, you best get him back.

*(**FRANK** disappears.)*

*(**GILLESPIE** hangs up and crosses to –)*

(blackout)

Scene Fourteen

(Police station lobby. **TIBBS** *on the phone as* **GILLESPIE** *enters.)*

TIBBS. Yes, sir. Actually I was hoping to leave by – Yes, sir, but…I…Yes…I understand.

(Long pause, he makes eye contact with **GILLESPIE**, *then:)*

Fine. Yes, sir.

*(***TIBBS*** *hangs up.)*

GILLESPIE. Who you yappin' to, Virgil?

TIBBS. Chief Morris in Pasadena.

GILLESPIE. He wishin' you well on vacation?

TIBBS. I think you know.

GILLESPIE. Then we both got the good news?

TIBBS. I wouldn't call it that.

GILLESPIE. Endicott's a big dog with a loud bark. Best way to deal with this: Hang back, stay outta my way, and when I need you, I'll give you a shout. We clear?

TIBBS. Not even close.

GILLESPIE. Come again?

TIBBS. If Chief Morris wants me here I'm gonna do my job, just like I would at home.

GILLESPIE. 'Cept this ain't your home. This ain't Pasadena. I doubt you could find your own goddamn shoes here if they weren't on your feet.

TIBBS. Started my career in Watts. I went to Pasadena for an opportunity I wasn't getting in L.A. I doubt there's anything here I've never seen.

GILLESPIE. You got snakes in L.A. Rattlers, yeah?

TIBBS. Sure do.

GILLESPIE. We got our pit vipers. About three different types of rattler…diamondbacks…but add to that your Cottonmouths for good measure…One minute you're walkin' down the street, next minute you're sittin' up on a cloud singin' one a' them nice gospel hymns, no idea what bit 'ya.

TIBBS. A snake's a snake.

GILLESPIE. Then you ain't as smart as I've been givin' you credit for.

TIBBS. Then maybe I'll just go catch my train…

GILLESPIE. Your boss says you're mine for a week. You gonna defy your Chief?

TIBBS. He'll understand.

GILLESPIE. And I'll make sure he don't.

(*beat, a change in tone*)

Goddamnit, Virgil, I got 'em takin' bites outta me from every direction here…

TIBBS. Then don't talk to me about hanging back.

GILLESPIE. Fine! Do the job you wanna do. But you keep me tied in.

(*beat*)

TIBBS. We should talk with Tatum's daughter and Endicott in more detail. Do you know anything about this other man who works for Tatum?

GILLESPIE. Kaufman?

TIBBS. Yeah.

GILLESPIE. Not a goddamn thing.

TIBBS. We'll talk with him as well.

GILLESPIE. Best get settled first.

TIBBS. There a hotel nearby?

GILLESPIE. Not one that'll take you. But there's a place for coloreds about five miles up the road.

TIBBS. I'll need my own transportation.

GILLESPIE. No you won't. You need to get anywhere, Sam'll drive you or you can walk. And you won't be wearing a uniform either.

TIBBS. I haven't had to wear a uniform in a long, long time. Being a detective, I mean.

(*Long pause,* **GILLESPIE** *just looking at* **TIBBS**.)

GILLESPIE Right…

(*Lights shift to:*)

Scene Fifteen

(The Endicott House.
(TIBBS, SAM, MELANIE, ENDICOTT, ERIC KAUFMAN,
30s, Mr. Tatum's business associate.)

TIBBS. Mr. Kaufman...it's important to know everyone's whereabouts. Now, what time did you leave your meeting with Mr. Tatum and Mr. Endicott?

KAUFMAN. You know, I'm not sure I like your tone.

TIBBS. It's just a question.

KAUFMAN. Well, watch yourself and remember who you are.

TIBBS. I promise, I never forget. *(beat)* Now...last night?

(pause)

KAUFMAN. Had to leave at ten in order to drive to Birmingham.

TIBBS. All night?

KAUFMAN. Got there at two-thirty in the morning. Checked into a hotel to get some sleep. Was up shaving when the call came through.

*(***TIBBS*** turns to ***MELANIE***. His voice changes slightly, softening just a touch –)*

TIBBS. Ms. Tatum, were there any landowners or partners in the deal that might have been angry with your father?

MELANIE. All the buy-outs he made were fair as far as I knew. He certainly wasn't pressuring anyone.

TIBBS. Did your father carry considerable sums of money with him?

MELANIE. Just for travelling expenses and such. I tried to get him to use travellers checks, but...he found them too much bother.

(beat)

Was that what he was...killed for? A few hundred dollars?

TIBBS. We don't know.

(**MELANIE** *stands up –*)

MELANIE. I'd like to go outside for a little while. I know it's hot, but, please, I need some air.

KAUFMAN. Now hold on. You're not going out there alone. We're isolated up here, but until this is cleared up, I don't want to take any chances – none whatsoever.

(**SAM** *stands up –*)

SAM WOOD. I'll go with her.

KAUFMAN. I'm perfectly capable –

TIBBS. I need you here.

KAUFMAN. Excuse me?

TIBBS. I'm not done talking to you.

SAM WOOD. I'll escort Ms. Tatum.

ENDICOTT. Thank you.

(**KAUFMAN** *bristles at this but holds his tongue.*)

(**SAM** *and* **MELANIE** *move outside as lights shift with them.*)

(*Outside.*

KAUFMAN *watches* **SAM** *and* **MELANIE** *from the window.*)

MELANIE. My mother passed away when I was young. My father did the best he could. He sacrificed…many things…for me. I'm his only child. His only legacy.

(**SAM** *nods, not sure what to say. But then,* **MELANIE** *asks what is really on her mind:*)

Was it…instantaneous?

SAM WOOD. I'm sure. No pain. He had no knowledge of… anything.

(**MELANIE**'s *strong, tries to hold back tears, but she can't. She takes a moment to compose herself.*)

MELANIE. Charles wanted to help this town. Yes, he wanted to make money, but…to him…his work was more than that. It was bringing people opportunity…modern conveniences. He wasn't a perfect man. But he had a good heart. And he had a vision of how to make…

towns like this...into better places. He had a vision on how to take a dying city...and help it thrive again.

(beat)

MELANIE. *(cont.)* Whoever killed my father killed his hopes. His dreams. And they killed all the good he was planning on bringing to this town.

(Again, **MELANIE** *breaks down, but this time she hugs* **SAM***, burying her face in his chest.* **SAM** *doesn't know what to do...awkwardly holds her...patting her back.)*

SAM WOOD. Ms. Tatum...everyone in the police department is gonna do our best, no matter how hard we have to work, to find and punish whoever did this. That isn't much comfort, but it might help a little.

MELANIE. You're a kind man, Mr. Wood. Are you a family man?

SAM WOOD. No. Why you ask?

MELANIE. You just seem...adept at...making a person feel calm. Like you've had experience...

(doesn't know how to finish what she's saying in the right way...)

...well, I guess...giving comfort comes with your job.

SAM WOOD. Sometimes...

(Hold the moment between them, then:)

(Back in the house, **TIBBS** *continues questioning* **KAUFMAN** *– and he's getting pissed.)*

KAUFMAN. There's only so much of this I'm going to put up with Mr. Endicott. I will not be interrogated or questioned by a man like this.

TIBBS. We need to establish where everyone was last night. It's crucial to the investigation that –

KAUFMAN. – What more do you want? I've told you five times already!

TIBBS. You need to relax.

KAUFMAN. Don't tell me what I need to do, boy!

(**KAUFMAN** *shoves* **TIBBS** –)

(*But* **TIBBS** *quickly gets* **KAUFMAN**'s *arm into a submission hold.*)

ENDICOTT. Easy! Hey, now !

KAUFMAN. Get…off me…

TIBBS. I said relax. And when I say that, I mean it.

(**TIBBS** *lets go.*
KAUFMAN *pulls away, rubbing his arm.*
SAM *sees this.* **SAM** *and* **MELANIE** *rush in* –)

SAM WOOD. Virgil! What 'n the hell's going on here?

KAUFMAN. He attacked me!

TIBBS. He took a swing. I defended myself.

KAUFMAN. This son-of-a-bitch came at –

ENDICOTT. Eric, shut up.

(*beat*)

I apologize for Mr. Kaufman's behavior. He's been working with us on this project for a long time and everything that's happened is fraying all our nerves.

TIBBS. Yes, well, that's…understandable.

SAM WOOD. Virgil, I think it's time we left.

(**SAM** *and* **TIBBS** *head for the door.*)

MELANIE. Mr. Wood?

SAM WOOD. Yes, Ma'am?

MELANIE. Please. If you find out anything. Anything at all… I'd appreciate it if you'd contact me personally. Keep me informed.

SAM WOOD. You can count on that.

(**SAM** *and* **TIBBS** *exit.*)

(**KAUFMAN**, **ENDICOTT** *and* **MELANIE** *disappear.*)

What the hell happened in there?

TIBBS. Exactly what I told you.

SAM WOOD. You might think about treading lighter in these parts.

TIBBS. One thing I know, Sam, some people you can't tread light enough. Ever. No matter what you do. They're gonna think and do what they want. One sure way to mess everything up is to try and placate people like that.

SAM WOOD. Placate?

TIBBS. Some people, they just wanna hate. I figure let 'em. It gives me an advantage.

(**SAM** *ponders this.*)

SAM WOOD. I'm gettin' a bit hungry. Maybe we should get some food.

TIBBS. What's your take on Oberst?

SAM WOOD. I ain't surprised he's in trouble again if that's what you mean?

TIBBS. Again?

SAM WOOD. Oh, yeah. He got squirrely with a local girl named Noreen Purdy a little while back.

(**TIBBS** *nods. Thinks for a long beat.*)

TIBBS. When we're done eating, we're gonna have another chat with Oberst.

(**SAM** *nods, drives, but looks a bit unsettled…*)

(*Lights shift to:*)

Scene Sixteen

(Diner parking lot)

*(**RALPH**, the waiter/counter man at the diner, is dumping trash when **TIBBS** and **SAM** approach.)*

RALPH. Evening, Sam.

SAM WOOD. That's Mr. Woods.

RALPH. Oh, right. Guess I forgot.

*(**SAM** heads inside. **TIBBS** behind him.)*

RALPH. Hey-hey, now, where you think you're going?

*(**SAM** and **TIBBS** turn.)*

RALPH. We don't serve your kind, fella.

TIBBS. I'm a police officer…

RALPH. I don't give a shit who you are, you ain't steppin' foot inside and I sure as shit ain't gonna serve you.

*(**RALPH** almost wilts under **TIBBS'** glare.)*

RALPH. Sam, you gonna curb yer boy?

SAM WOOD. Don't worry about it. I'll bring you out something.

TIBBS. Just want a drink…

SAM WOOD. You know how it is.

TIBBS. Right…

SAM WOOD. What can I get ya?

TIBBS. Forget it.

SAM WOOD. Virgil…

TIBBS. I'll be at the car.

*(**TIBBS** exits.)*

(Lights shift to The Diner.
PETE *is there, off duty, having dinner.*
SAM *comes in and sits.*
RALPH *goes behind the counter.)*

RALPH. Shit, can you imagine that? The hell he think he is?

PETE. I told you, they gonna come and do their sit-ins and protests here sooner or later.

RALPH. Let 'em. I'll teach 'em why God made rope and strong tree branches.

(**PETE** *laughs at that.*)

SAM WOOD. I'll take some of that pie and a coffee.

PETE. Pete likes 'im.

RALPH. The nigger?

SAM WOOD. Shut the fuck up, Pete.

RALPH. This true, Sam?

SAM WOOD. How many times I gotta tell you when I'm on duty –

RALPH. Mr. Woods.

SAM WOOD. That's right.

RALPH. So 'sit true?

SAM WOOD. He ain't that bad.

PETE. See!

SAM WOOD. Damn smart for a colored boy.

RALPH. And my dog's smart for a dog, but that don't make him too smart does it?

(*Again,* **PETE** *cackles at that.*
SAM *lets it go.*)

RALPH. What's new with the investigation?

SAM WOOD. It's goin'.

RALPH. You know who done it yet?

SAM WOOD. Not yet.

RALPH. Got any clues or some such…?

SAM WOOD. Why don't you ask Pete?

RALPH. Pete don't know nothin'.

PETE. I know all I gotta know and if I don't know it I don't need it.

SAM WOOD. I'm not talkin' about police business.

RALPH. Fine, fine…just being nosey.

SAM WOOD. Well can it. Give me some milk but save it for when I leave.

RALPH. No problem.

(**RALPH** *busies himself with the order.*)

PETE. Ralph, don't you got something to talk to Sam about?

RALPH. Yeah, actually, I kinda do…

SAM WOOD. *(not too interested)* What would that be?

RALPH. You know, I was thinking about the night…

SAM WOOD. Which one?

RALPH. Of the murder…

SAM WOOD. Yeah?

PETE. He remembered something. I told 'im to go into the station after work but here you are…

RALPH. Yeah. I remembered somethin' I forgot to tell you about.

SAM WOOD. Which is what?

RALPH. What time you guys say the murder took place?

SAM WOOD. Just tell me what you wanna tell me, Ralph.

RALPH. Okay. Well. I saw this pink Pontiac driving through right around…I'd say around two.

SAM WOOD. That a fact?

RALPH. Yeah.

SAM WOOD. And you didn't remember a pink Pontiac before?

RALPH. Well I did, but I didn't remember to tell you about it.

SAM WOOD. And why's that?

RALPH. Well…just didn't think about it. Too much excitement I guess. And I thought you caught the guy – Oberst.

PETE. C'mon, everyone knows Ralph here can't keep more'n three things in his head at once.

RALPH. Shut up, Pete.

(Pause. **RALPH** *works.* **PETE** *finishes his coffee.*)

RALPH. So you gonna tell Gillespie about it?

SAM WOOD. Most likely.

 (**PETE** *gets up.*)

PETE. That's it for me. I'm hitting the hay. I'll leave the rest of the evening to you night owls.

 (**PETE** *exits.*)

 (**RALPH** *serves* **SAM** *the food.*)

RALPH. Can I ask you something?

SAM WOOD. I'd rather you just let me eat.

RALPH. Does he smell? I mean, being stuck in the car with the black boy? Does he smell?

SAM WOOD. Ralph?

RALPH. Yeah…?

SAM WOOD. Get the fuck away from me and let me eat.

RALPH. Sorry…

SAM WOOD. Now.

 (**RALPH** *slinks to the other end of the bar.*
 SAM *eats.*
 Lights shift.)

Scene Seventeen

(**HARVEY OBERST**'s cell.
SAM opens the cell door and **TIBBS** enters.)

OBERST. Aw, man! Get him outta here!

SAM WOOD. He wants to talk to you.

OBERST. Well, I sure as shit don't wanna talk to him.

(**SAM** exits.)

OBERST. Hey! Get back here!

(**TIBBS** sits on one of the bunks.
OBERST stares at Tibbs.
TIBBS doesn't say anything for a long while.
OBERST fidgets.
Finally –)

OBERST. What you doin' with white man's clothes on, boy?

TIBBS. What makes them white man's clothes if I'm wearing 'em?

OBERST. You been to school?

TIBBS. College.

OBERST. Think you're smart or something?

TIBBS. I graduated.

OBERST. Where'd they let you go to college?

TIBBS. California.

OBERST. Out there they don't care what they do.

(beat)

Who the hell you think you are?

TIBBS. A cop.

OBERST. Don't lie to me, nigger.

TIBBS. I'm the only one who thinks you might not be guilty of murder, so maybe you watch how you talk to me.

OBERST. And maybe I don't.

(beat)

TIBBS. Deputy Wood mentioned you got in a problem not too long ago.

OBERST. Maybe.

TIBBS. Who's Noreen Purdy?

OBERST. A white girl. Means she ain't none'a your business.

TIBBS. Either you answer my questions, or take your chances gettin' executed for murder.

OBERST. I wanna talk to a real cop.

TIBBS. Son, I'm as real as they get.

(pause)

OBERST. Noreen lives near where I do. Sixteen. Almost seventeen.

TIBBS. In California, we call that San Quentin tail.

OBERST. I got in trouble with her, but not that way.

TIBBS. Go on...

(no response)

I can go look up the record. Rather get it from you.

OBERST. This Noreen, she's young but real stacked, if you know what I mean. A real hot sweater-girl type.

TIBBS. There're lots of those.

OBERST. Yeah, but this Noreen's real proud a' what nature done for her in the upstairs area of her chest region. She likes to show 'em off. I took her on a date to Clark's Pond. We weren't plannin' nothing wrong. I don't wanna join no chain gang, fuck no. Anyhow, she asks me if I don't think she's got a nice figure, and when I say yes, she decides to show me. And I'll be goddamned if she didn't just whip that shirt off and let them beauties come out to play.

TIBBS. Her idea?

OBERST. Damn right. Like you said, her idea. I didn't mess her up or nothin' like that. I just didn't try'n stop her.

TIBBS. Not too many people would blame you for that, but it's pretty dangerous.

OBERST. Maybe. Anyhow, she gets half undressed and right
then a cop comes outta the bushes. I get hauled in.

TIBBS. How 'bout the girl?

OBERST. Sent home.

TIBBS. And after that?

OBERST. After a while they let me go. Told me never mess
with her no more.

TIBBS. Seen her since?

OBERST. See her all the time. Lives on Third at the corner
of Polk. I live a block from there. And she wants
another date. What'm I supposed to do? Jesus…

TIBBS. That's all that happened?

OBERST. So help me.

(**TIBBS** *stands. Stares at him a long moment.* **OBERST**
gets fidgety.)

What…?

TIBBS. You shave every day?

OBERST. Usually. Not this morning. Been up all night.

TIBBS. How come?

OBERST. Went to Springville to see a guy. We had a couple
of dates.

TIBBS. Got back pretty late then?

OBERST. Around two. Maybe later. That's when I found the
guy in the road.

TIBBS. Don't tell me what you think I want to hear. Exactly
what did you do?

OBERST. Well…this here guy's laying in the road. I get out
to see if I could help him. He was dead.

TIBBS. How'd you know?

OBERST. Just knew s'all. Ain't nothin' in nature as still as a
dead man.

TIBBS. True enough…

OBERST. Then I seen his wallet lying on the road. 'bout
four or five feet from him.

TIBBS. That's very important. I don't care whether you found the wallet or whether you took it from his pocket, it makes no difference. But are you absolutely sure you found it on the road beside him?

OBERST. I swear.

TIBBS. And after that?

OBERST. Picked it up, looked inside, saw a lot of money. Figured he couldn't use it, and if I left it there, whoever came along next would grab it.

TIBBS. How'd you get caught with it on you?

OBERST. Got worried on account of the guy'd been killed. Anyone finds me with the wallet, I'm fucked. So I go to see Mr. Jennings. He's head man at the bank. I know him 'cause I work for him on weekends. Told him about it. Said it'd have to be reported and he called the cops. But then I got scared and ran...

(*beat*)

TIBBS. Okay...Leave it to me.

(**TIBBS** *exits.*)

OBERST. Where you going? What's next? Hey! Get back here, boy! You get back here!!

(*Lights shift to:*)

Scene Eighteen

(Gillespie's office. **TIBBS** *enters –)*

GILLESPIE. What is it?

TIBBS. You need to release Oberst.

GILLESPIE. Now why would that be?

TIBBS. Technically you can hold him for grand theft, but I checked with Jennings at the bank. He confirms Oberst's story. With a responsible citizen to testify, you'd never get a conviction.

GILLESPIE. You a strange one, Tibbs. Every time I think I got you figured out, you're on to some other bit of strangeness.

TIBBS. How's that?

GILLESPIE. You seem to spend more time gettin' em out of jail than you do tryin' to put 'em in.

TIBBS. Maybe I wanna make sure there's plenty of room when I get the right one.

(beat)

GILLESPIE. *(long moment)* Say I do…he's your responsibility.

TIBBS. Fine.

GILLESPIE. Can you live with that?…If he does somethin' else?

TIBBS. Guess I'd have to.

(beat)

GILLESPIE. Still looks like a good suspect to me.

TIBBS. Not everything's how it looks.

GILLESPIE. What's the progress then? If you're gettin' rid of who we got, you damn sure better have some idea who you plan to put in.

TIBBS. Got some leads…

GILLESPIE. And?

TIBBS. I'm following them.

GILLESPIE. What are they?

TIBBS. If they amount to anything, I'll tell you.

GILLESPIE. Tell me what you got now, when I ask for it.

TIBBS. I'll tell you what I got when I think it'll be worth both our time.

GILLESPIE. I want the fucking information now! Don't you start thinking you can stand there face-to-face and sass me! Now I heard you talked to that fella Ralph tipped you on – in the pink Caddy?

TIBBS. That's right.

GILLESPIE. And?

TIBBS. I sent him on his way.

GILLESPIE. Yeah, I know that.

TIBBS. So what's the problem here?

GILLESPIE. He was at the scene of the crime…

TIBBS. …True.

GILLESPIE. No other cars were seen!

TIBBS. That's right…

GILLESPIE. The doctor fixed the time of death at the very moment Ralph fingered the man as driving through town. And you clear him?

TIBBS. All reasonable points, Chief, and I'd agree completely except for one thing.

GILLESPIE. Which is?

TIBBS. Tatum wasn't killed where his body was found.

(Hold a moment, then – blackout.)

Scene Nineteen

(Red police lights.
Night. **KAUFMAN** *in his car. He's just been pulled over.*
SAM *approaches the window.)*

SAM WOOD. What're you doin' this hour?

KAUFMAN. On my way to Birmingham.

SAM WOOD. This the time you usually start trips?

KAUFMAN. That any business of yours?

*(***SAM***'s hand moves to his sidearm.)*

SAM WOOD. Everything's my business when we got a murderer loose.

KAUFMAN. You don't have to remind me.

SAM WOOD. Ain't you worried someone might be gunnin' for you?

KAUFMAN. It's crossed my mind.

SAM WOOD. Where you comin' from?

KAUFMAN. I was up at the Endicotts' discussing what we're gonna do about the development. Who we're gonna get to take Tatum's place that isn't gonna make our investors turn tail and run.

SAM WOOD. So you're still going through with it?

KAUFMAN. Got no choice. Unless we wanna loose our shirts on the money we've already put into this. If we don't keep things on track, we'll all be dead. I'm sorry – that's a bad choice of words.

(He collect himself.)

Anyhow, I've got to go to Birmingham and see what we can come up with.

SAM WOOD. According to the story you told me and Virgil, you didn't get much sleep last night. Can't be in good condition to drive.

KAUFMAN. Life's tough all over, isn't it.

SAM WOOD. How's everything at the Endicott's?

KAUFMAN. Strained.

SAM WOOD. Melanie's holding up okay?

KAUFMAN. You don't worry yourself about Melanie.

SAM WOOD. Maybe I'll swing by and check on her myself.

KAUFMAN. How can you put up with this shit?

SAM WOOD. What's that?

KAUFMAN. Followin' the black boy like he's your boss.

SAM WOOD. He ain't my boss.

KAUFMAN. Sure seems that way.

SAM WOOD. Well he ain't, and don't make me tell you again.

KAUFMAN. Now, do you have to check with the black boy or are you gonna let me keep on driving?

(**SAM** *steps back.*)

SAM WOOD. Get outta here. And get off the road as soon as you can. Don't want you ending up in the morgue alongside your boss.

(*Lights shift to:*)

Scene Twenty

(Mayor's Office. **GILLESPIE,** **MAYOR SHUBERT***)*

SCHUBERT. I'm concerned about your investigation.

GILLESPIE. Concerned how?

SCHUBERT. You got Tibbs running around town askin' questions of white people like he thinks he's somebody. Then he's down at the bank acting like he's a white man. A few of the boys're gettin' ready to teach him his place, and they will, if you don't get his ass outta here. I got all kinds of people on the phone screaming at me, and I wanna know what you're doing about it.

GILLESPIE. Hold on just a goddamn second: I didn't want Tibbs involved. Now why you playin' games with me, Frank?

SCHUBERT. We got a murder here. That's no game. And as far as I know, at least for the time being, you're still the Sheriff, right?

*(***GILLESPIE*** stares.)*

Ain't you still the sheriff?

GILLESPIE. That's right.

SCHUBERT. So then if there's a murderer running loose, that'd be your problem, right? Right, Frank?

GILLESPIE. That's right.

SCHUBERT. So don't be tryin' to muddy the waters with who said what. You're the final authority on what happens under your roof.

*(***SCHUBERT*** reaches into his desk, produces a small bundle of newspapers.)*

I got a phone call from *Newsweek.* Wanted a full rundown on our use of Tibbs. If they run it, that means national publicity whether we want it or not. And I for one don't want it.

(beat)

I'm not trying to put turpentine on your tail, but are you gonna get us out of this anytime soon?

GILLESPIE. There's a routine for this sort of thing, a routine that gets results. We're following it. I'm keeping Virgil under control and if he gets one bit out of line, I'll slap him down hard. I know he was at the bank, but so far he hasn't done anything I can pin him for.

SCHUBERT. Lots of people read *Newsweek.* I do. I don't want this situation blowing up on us. We gotta ride this out. Last thing we want is a lot of hassles, 'specially with an election on the horizon. I want this man gone before the boys get impatient and rough him up. A black boy swinging from a tree, and we got the FBI down here.

(**GILLESPIE** *and* **SCHUBERT** *lock eyes.*)

SCHUBERT. Are we seeing things eye-to-eye?

GILLESPIE. More or less.

SCHUBERT. Go catch us that murderer.

(*Lights shift to:*)

Scene Twenty-one

(Police Office. **SAM** *and* **PETE***)*

SAM WOOD. Get offa my back! I'm not askin', I'm tellin'!

PETE. Jesus, Sam, listen to you!

SAM WOOD. Not another word, hear me?

PETE. Actin' like he's your new friend.

SAM WOOD. Didn't say 'nothin' like that.

PETE. Think maybe you wanna make this coon yer partner. You gettin' lonely patrolling all night?

*(***SAM*** *grabs* ***PETE*** *by the shirt, slams him into the wall.)*

SAM WOOD. Goddamnit, Pete, you want me to take you out back? 'Cause I sure as hell will.

PETE. Okay, okay, fine –

(pushes **SAM** *away)*

– Relax goddammit! Shit!

SAM WOOD. Maybe you can't tell, but I ain't in the mood.

PETE. Fine, so you ain't in the mood. Now I ain't in the mood either, how you like that?

SAM WOOD. I said he had guts. That's all.

PETE. Everyone's got a right to have their own mind about things.

SAM WOOD. Good.

PETE. Still...don't see why you think he's got guts, just 'cause he handled a body. His job, ain't it? Not like the damn thing's gonna get up and bite him.

(trying for a joke)

'Less he believes in voodoo!

*(***TIBBS*** *appears at the door.)*

TIBBS. Excuse me, could you tell me where I can wash?

PETE. Colored washroom's down the hall to your right.

SAM WOOD. *(to* **PETE***)* No soap down there.

PETE. That's what he's got a shirttail for.

*(***TIBBS*** *exits down the hallway.*
A silent moment between ***PETE*** *and* ***SAM*** *regarding* ***TIBBS***, *then –)*

Scene Twenty-two

(**TIBBS** *and* **SAM** *in the patrol car. Night.*)

TIBBS. As closely as you can, do exactly as you did the night Tatum was killed. Try to follow the same route and at the same speed. Can you do that?

SAM WOOD. I won't miss the time by five minutes.

TIBBS. Perfect.

(*They drive in silence. Time passes.*)

SAM WOOD. Learnin' anything?

TIBBS. Mostly how hot it gets in the middle of the night.

(*beat*)

You go through the FBI school?

SAM WOOD. No chance to.

(*silence*)

I wanna ask you something.

TIBBS. Go ahead.

SAM WOOD. Maybe this ain't my business, but I hear you told Gillespie somethin' that shook 'im bad.

TIBBS. And?

SAM WOOD. Sure like to know what it was.

TIBBS. Tatum wasn't killed where you found him.

SAM WOOD. No shit?

TIBBS. His body was dumped there.

SAM WOOD. How the hell you know this?

TIBBS. When I examined the body.

SAM WOOD. How's that?

TIBBS. The palms of his hands.

SAM WOOD. Suppose you take it from the top.

TIBBS. Let's go back to the moment Tatum was hit on the head. We know now it was a fatal blow. But it isn't clear whether the man died instantly or was still conscious for at least a few seconds after he was struck. Now if he died instantly, what would happen?

SAM WOOD. He'd fall down.

TIBBS. But how?

SAM WOOD. Like a sack of potatoes.

TIBBS. Unconscious or dead, his knees would unlock, shoulders would sag. His head would fall forward – he'd be more or less in a heap.

SAM WOOD. But Tatum's body was spread out...his hands were over his head.

TIBBS. That's right.

SAM WOOD. Wait – supposed he was still conscious a few seconds after he was hit...

TIBBS. ...keep going...

SAM WOOD. ...then he'd throw out his arms and try to save himself...

TIBBS. You're sounding like a homicide detective...

SAM WOOD. – and that's the way I found him.

TIBBS. Yep.

SAM WOOD. So he was conscious after he was hit.

TIBBS. *(shakes his head "no")* Supposed Tatum was hit where you found him. For his body to spread out that way, he'd try and break his fall with his hands...

SAM WOOD. The pavement would've scratched his hands, taken off some skin...

TIBBS. So...?

SAM WOOD. No skin off the palms, no marks like that, it wasn't where he fell...

TIBBS. ...or if it was, someone was careful to spread the body out afterwards.

SAM WOOD. Which isn't likely...

TIBBS. Why?

SAM WOOD. It was the middle of the road, a car could've come along at any time. I could've.

TIBBS. You got the makings of a professional.

(They drive...lights transition and sounds rise...as if they're traveling around the city and some time is passing. Then –)

SAM WOOD. Virgil.

TIBBS. Yeah, Sam.

SAM WOOD. I wanna ask you something you ain't gonna like. But I wanna know.

TIBBS. Go ahead.

SAM WOOD. How'd they take you as a cop? How a colored man get all those advantages? If you wanna get mad, go ahead...

TIBBS. You've always lived in the South?

SAM WOOD. Born, raised, and damn proud of it.

TIBBS. There are places where I go weeks without anyone bringing up the color of my skin. Here, I can't go fifteen minutes. If you went somewhere and people despised you because your southern accent, and you were just speaking naturally you might have an idea what it's like being hated for something shouldn't make any difference anyhow.

SAM WOOD. Some guys down here'd kill you for saying a thing like that.

TIBBS. You've made my point.

(They drive.)

SAM WOOD. Got yourself a girl?

TIBBS. Had one.

SAM WOOD. What happened?

TIBBS. Probably the same things you've encountered.

SAM WOOD. What d'you mean?

TIBBS. You're single.

SAM WOOD. Yeah...So?

TIBBS. This job eats up a lot of time, but more than that, a lot of your thinking. A lotta other parts as well. She found herself someone where that wasn't a problem.

SAM WOOD. What's the new guy do? If you don't mind me askin'?

TIBBS. Milkman.

SAM WOOD. Milkman?

TIBBS. Got dumped for a milkman.

(A beat, then they both smile.)

For some reason, him being a milkman took some of the sting out of it. Not sure why, but it did.

(Maybe they share a laugh...
A beat of more driving. Lights and sound transition.
They come to a stop and get out.)

How on time are you?

SAM WOOD. To the minute.

TIBBS. You've been a help. More than you may realize.

SAM WOOD. No problem, Virgil. My job.

TIBBS. Now I wanna ask one more thing...

*(**SAM** shrugs: sure.)*

TIBBS. Why'd you change your route when we were across the tracks a little while ago.

*(**SAM** tenses.)*

SAM WOOD. What're you talkin' about.

TIBBS. You said you'd take me the exact same route.

SAM WOOD. And I did.

TIBBS. No. You didn't.

SAM WOOD. And I'm tellin' you I did.

TIBBS. You're lying, Sam.

SAM WOOD. You watch yourself, Virgil. I like you, but don't you dare talk to me like that.

TIBBS. Then tell me the truth.

SAM WOOD. I told you all I'm gonna tell you.

TIBBS. Why're you lying?

SAM WOOD. Get the fuck outta my car.

TIBBS. Sam!

SAM WOOD. Don't make me throw you out!

*(**TIBBS** gets out of the car.*
***SAM** and his car disappears. We hear the car drive away.*
***TIBBS** left alone in the dark.*
Lights shift to:)

Scene Twenty-three

(Lights rise on a man in shadows.)

MAN IN SHADOWS: Gillespie: Maybe you have wondered why you got the job here when a lot better men who would have taken the job were turned down. It's because you come from the South and we figured you were big enough to keep the niggers in their place. We don't want integration, we want you to keep the damn niggers out of our schools and every other place the nigger lovers want them to get. We don't want them neither in our police department. So get rid of that shine you got working for you and kick him out of town or else. If you don't we'll do it for you and we ain't kidding. If you don't, we'll run you out too, and you are not too big to be put in your place either. You have been warned.

(Enraged, **GILLESPIE** *crushes the letter in his fist...)*

Scene Twenty-four

(Road. Later that night.
TIBBS *walking.*
Headlights strobe over him.
We hear shouting…
"There he is."
"Well lookie here!"
Sound of a car pulling over. Gravel crunching under wheels.
TIBBS *looks around for something to use as a weapon as –*
THREE MEN *step from the dark. They are members of the Klu Klux Klan. They can either be wearing white sheets, burlap sacks as masks, or some other method of hiding their identities.*

KLAN #1. Where you goin' boy?

KLAN #2. You lost? Need a ride?

KLAN #3. Nigger town's that way. You're going the wrong direction, boy!

(They jump **TIBBS**.
TIBBS *gives better than he gets until sheer numbers take him down.*
TIBBS *slammed in the gut.* **TIBBS** *drops.* **KLAN #3** *runs to the car, brings back robe.)*

KLAN #1. You want a ride to town…we'll give you a ride. Only thing, we ain't got no room in the truck …

KLAN #2. Means you gotta take the Nigger Express….

KLAN #1. …this ride's gonna be a bit bumpy.

*(***TIBBS** *struggles as* **THE KLANSMEN** *laugh, kicking and tying* **TIBBS** *up.*
A new set of headlights appears.)

KLAN #2. Shit…

KLAN #1. Probably Cooper…

*(***THE KLANSMEN** *shield their eyes from the headlights.*
We hear a car door open and –
SAM *enters.)*

SAM WOOD. Get away – Step off there –

KLAN #1. How you doin' officer?

SAM WOOD. The hell you doing – Virgil, you okay – you, back!

KLAN #1. He's fine –

KLAN #2. I'm back, I'm back –

SAM WOOD. You dumb sons-a-bitches – Back away!

> *(They back away from* **TIBBS***.*
> **TIBBS** *struggles to his feet.)*

KLAN #2. We just givin' him a ride.

SAM WOOD. This man's on official police business.

KLAN #1. I don't care what he's on.

SAM WOOD. You had your fun.

KLAN #3. Not enough.

SAM WOOD. This ain't gonna be good for nobody.

KLAN #1. This shit ain't coming here. You know what I'm talkin' about, Sam. Don't act like you don't.

SAM WOOD. Move on home, boys.

KLAN #3. Gillespie thinks we gonna let a nigger cop run around town?

SAM WOOD. Ask him yourself. He's on his way.

KLAN #2. Bullshit.

> *(They move towards* **SAM** *and* **TIBBS***.*
> **SAM** *pulls his gun.)*

KLAN #3. We got guns too.

SAM WOOD. But mine's pulled…and aimed at your balls.

> *(Siren in the distance.)*

KLAN #1. You're worse than a nigger.

SAM WOOD. Maybe. Maybe not.

> *(They back away.)*

KLAN #1. Be seein' you. Be seein' all a' you.

> *(***THE KLANSMEN** *disappear into the night.*
> *The sound of the siren rises.*
> *Lights shift to:)*

Scene Twenty-five

(Gillespie's office.
GILLESPIE looks over the crime scene photos.
TIBBS enters. He has bandages for the cuts and bruises
he got in the fight.)

GILLESPIE. Everything okay?

TIBBS. Cuts and bruises.

GILLESPIE. Hell you doin' out there alone?

TIBBS. Sam and I had a disagreement.

GILLESPIE. Sam's a pretty agreeable sort. I'm surprised...

TIBBS. He mislead me on something, and when I commented on it he dropped me off without ceremony.

GILLESPIE. Misled you how?

TIBBS. Asked him to retrace the exact route he followed on the murder night...but at one point he made a slight deviation.

GILLESPIE. Virgil, you can't possibly expect the man to remember every turn he made on any specific night.

TIBBS. I wanted to know exactly where he was prior to the time he discovered the body. Which streets he drove.

GILLESPIE. That's important?

TIBBS. Could be.

(pause)

GILLESPIE. You be careful, you got me?

TIBBS. Of course.

GILLESPIE. Fine, then. That's it.

(TIBBS exits.
GILLESPIE thinks...
IN ANOTHER PLACE AND TIME: TATUM appears.
Alive.
It's night. TATUM walks down the street.
SAM appears from the darkness.
SAM says something to Tatum.
TATUM stops. They speak. TATUM turns around and
walks away.

SAM *eyes the street, takes out his baton and slams* TATUM *on the skull.*
TATUM *drops.*
SAM *hits him three more times.*
Pulls the wallet. Takes out money and throws the wallet down, and disappears.)

GILLESPIE. *(ponders the possibility)* No. Fuck no.
(Thinking some more, he looks at the doorway, as if somehow thinking of TIBBS.*)*

Sam. Sam...Shit.

*(*GILLESPIE *grabs his phone and calls* JENNINGS, *the banker.)*

JENNINGS. Bank of Argo, Al Jennings.

GILLESPIE. Jennings, Gillespie here. I gotta ask you something in strict confidence concerning one of our men. You know Sam Wood.

JENNINGS. Very well.

GILLESPIE. Within the last two months there been any unusual activity in his account? Deposits or withdrawals Borrowing money?

JENNINGS. Ordinarily we try to keep information concerning our depositors confidential. In any event, we don't like to give it out over the telephone. You can appreciate why.

GILLESPIE. That's all fine, but you didn't answer my question.

JENNINGS. Let me understand clearly, Mr. Gillespie. Is this an official request for information?

GILLESPIE. You can consider it that.

JENNINGS. Then of course we'll cooperate. If you come to my office I'll allow you to look at the records.

GILLESPIE. Can't you bring it over here?

JENNINGS. If you get a court order for us, otherwise it'd be much better if you could come here. We don't want our records out and we avoid making copies whenever possible...

GILLESPIE. Fine, fine, fine. I'll be over. Have it ready.

(**GILLESPIE** *hangs up.* **PETE** *enters.*)

PETE. Virgil says you want his report on Tatum's body.

GILLESPIE. What've you been sitting on it for?

PETE. Didn't think you wanted it.

GILLESPIE. YES I GODDAMN WANT IT!

(**PETE** *puts the file on his desk and scuttles out.*
GILLESPIE *looks it over.*
His phone rings –)

What?!

SCHUBERT. It's Frank. You gettin' anywhere with this problem of ours?

GILLESPIE. We're getting somewhere. And when I got something to tell you I'll call.

SCHUBERT. My phone's burning with people pissed to high heaven. When's this gonna be put to bed?

GILLESPIE. Let me run the investigation.

SCHUBERT. Well speed it up, goddammit! We need that black boy outta here.

GILLESPIE. I'm not sure about that...

SCHUBERT. About what...?

GILLESPIE. Tibbs. Gotta be honest, Frank, he's startin' to grow on me. Hell, I might even offer 'im a job here.

SCHUBERT. Best think about how you're talking to me.

GILLESPIE. Oh, I thought about it all right. Now fuck off and let me do my job!

(**GILLESPIE** *slams the phone down, then grabs his hat and exits.*
Lights shift to:)

Scene Twenty-six

(The bank. **GILLESPIE** *and* **JENNINGS**.*)*

JENNINGS. Mr. Wood's had an account with us for several years. It's never been more than a few hundred dollars. Deposits and withdrawals've been consistent for some time.

GILLESPIE. There any more?

JENNINGS. Two days ago, Mr. Wood came in, paid off the mortgage on his home.

GILLESPIE. Keep going.

JENNINGS. He deposited a check, stated it was a legacy he'd received in the mail. That plus a little over six-hundred in cash...

*(***GILLESPIE*** nods, the ramifications of the information sinking in.)*

Lights shift to:)

Scene Twenty-seven

(Lights slowly up. Late night.
TIBBS enters Gillespie's office. He carries a sack.
GILLESPIE seems shaken up about something...He's pouring himself some whisky.)

GILLESPIE. What is it? I ain't in the mood for bullshit.

(TIBBS lays a metal pipe on Gillespie's desk.)

Yeah? So what?

TIBBS. It's the murder weapon.

(beat)

(GILLESPIE examines the pipe. There's dried blood on it.)

GILLESPIE. How'd you find it?

TIBBS. Went to the project site. This is plumbing pipe from the building they're gonna tear down.

(GILLESPIE continues to look at the pipe, lost in a thought.
TIBBS shifts, uncomfortable.)

Something wrong?

GILLESPIE. *(re: the whisky)* Want a drink?

TIBBS. I'm okay...

GILLESPIE. Have a drink with me, Virgil.

(beat)

TIBBS. Fine.

(TIBBS sits. GILLESPIE pours him a drink.)

GILLESPIE. What're you doin' after all this?

TIBBS. Heading back home.

GILLESPIE. I mean after doing what you do. "Detecting."

TIBBS. Well. I got a few ideas but nothing rock solid. Maybe start my own business. Private eye maybe.

(GILLESPIE sips his drink. A long beat. Awkward.)

GILLESPIE. You got a lot of ambition.

TIBBS. Normal amount I'd say.

GILLESPIE. Be a different country if more of your people had your kind of gumption.

(TIBBS downs his drink and gets up.)

TIBBS. *(re: the drink)* Thanks for this.

GILLESPIE. Hey, hey, what's your problem?

TIBBS. Who do you think broke their backs building this country?

GILLESPIE. Whoa – Just tryin' to give you a fucking compliment!

TIBBS. I don't need any.

GILLESPIE. Settle down, Tibbs.

TIBBS. *(heading for the door)* See you in the morning.

GILLESPIE. Told you once we could run our own business down here, didn't I?

(Something in GILLESPIE's voice stops TIBBS in the doorway. He turns to GILLESPIE.)

TIBBS. So what if you did?

GILLESPIE. I personally arrested Tatum's murderer an hour ago.

(TIBBS reacts – can't help himself, taking a quick breath, then –)

TIBBS. You got a confession?

GILLESPIE. No...I didn't. But he did it.

(turning the pipe over in his hands, examining it)

What did this tell you?

TIBBS. It confirmed what I knew.

GILLESPIE. Which is what?

TIBBS. Who the murderer is.

GILLESPIE. Well, I beat you to it. Didn't expect that did you?

(pause)

You'll find him in the first cell down the hall. It's your friend, Sam Wood.

*(A dim pool of light rises on **SAM** sitting in the cell.)*

TIBBS. Sam...?

*(**TIBBS** looks at **GILLESPIE**, stunned. He takes a moment to collect his thoughts –*
***TIBBS** has to sit.)*

GILLESPIE. I said we know what we were doing and I goddamn meant it. Don't matter where the trail leads, we follow it, we get justice. Take that back to Pasadena, tell him how it's done in the South.

*(**PETE** enters.)*

PETE. Sir, we got a complaint you should hear. I mean, I'm sure of it. Want me t'bring 'em in?

GILLESPIE. Yeah.

*(**PURDY** and **NOREEN** enter.)*

PURDY. Get 'im outta here. I ain't talkin' 'bout this with one'a them in the room.

GILLESPIE. He's staying where he is. What's the problem?

(pause)

PURDY. My daughter's been got into trouble.

GILLESPIE. The usual kind?

PURDY. 'Fraid so.

GILLESPIE. How old are you, Noreen.

NOREEN. Sixteen.

PURDY. That ain't exactly right. You see, Noreen, she was sick for a while and got behind in school. Kids is awful hard on somebody who ain't as far as she ought to be, so we let it out Noreen was fifteen when we moved here a year past.

GILLESPIE. But she's not?

PURDY. She was seventeen then, so that makes her just eighteen now.

GILLESPIE. Makes a big different. In this state a girl of sixteen gets in the family way, that's statutory rape.

PURDY. Unless she's married.

GILLESPIE. That's right. But if she's eighteen or over, and gives her consent, then it's fornication.

PURDY. What's that?

GILLESPIE. The business. But it's a lot less serious.

PURDY. What if some guy takes an innocent girl like my Noreen and smooth-talks her into doin' what she hadn't oughta. Ain't that the rape?

GILLESPIE. That's seduction.

PURDY. What's the goddamn difference?

GILLESPIE. Suppose you both sit down and tell me just what happened.

PURDY. Well, Noreen, she's a real good girl, never done nothin' wrong 'cept what kids always do. Then, with out me knowin' nothing about it, she meets this here guy twice as old as she is. He ain't married so he starts sniffin' around my girl like a horny mutt.

GILLESPIE. Shoulda stopped it.

PURDY. Mister, I work all night. Ain't got no time to stay home an' take care a'the kids or see what they's doin' every minute. Besides, Noreen didn't tell me nothing 'till afterwards.

NOREEN. I couldn't see nothing wrong in it.

GILLESPIE. When'd it happen?

PURDY. Real late one night. The missus was asleep like she oughta be, when Noreen got outta bed to see this guy, and that's when he had her.

GILLESPIE. Tell me about it; exactly what happened.

NOREEN. Well, like Pa said, he was real nice to me. We talked and then we sat real close together and then...

GILLESPIE. Did this man force himself on you so you had to struggle...or did it just work out he went farther than he should?

NOREEN. I didn't rightly understand everything at the time.

(*pause*)

GILLESPIE. All right, Noreen, this man did you wrong, of course, and we'll arrest him for it. We can charge him with seduction and that's plenty. Now tell me about him.

NOREEN. You know him right enough, it's that night cop you got out supposed to be protectin' the women all the time.

PURDY. It's that goddamn Sam Wood.

GILLESPIE. Wait a second now.

PURDY. It's your man did this, Chief! Your own goddamn man!

(TIBBS *slips out of the room.*)

GILLESPIE. Now, you're sure....

NOREEN. He's always been sweet on me. Do you blame him?

PURDY. Noreen...

GILLESPIE. Jesus Christ...

(GILLESPIE *notices* TIBBS *is gone. He hits the intercom –*)

Where's Virgil? What's he doing? Get his ass back in here.

PETE'S VOICE. He just stormed out. Took Sam's patrol car. Said something about being the biggest fool in the country and beat it outta here like he found the cure for being black.

(*Lights shift to:*)

Scene Twenty-eight

(The Endicott home. **TIBBS** *and* **ENDICOTT**.*)*

TIBBS. I wanna ask some questions I should've thought of long ago. Due to events down in the city, they're now extremely urgent.

ENDICOTT. Fine.

TIBBS. On the night Mr. Tatum was killed, he was up here earlier in the evening?

ENDICOTT. That's right.

TIBBS. Who was the first person to leave the house?

ENDICOTT. Mr. Kaufmann.

TIBBS. What time did he leave?

ENDICOTT. Can't be too exact...Don't believe anyone was paying close attention. Around Ten or so...

TIBBS. Exactly who was here?

ENDICOTT. Tatum – his daughter Melanie, my wife and myself...and Mr. Kaufman.

TIBBS. Can you estimate the time Tatum left?

ENDICOTT. Eleven – eleven-thirty.

TIBBS. How'd he get to the city?

ENDICOTT. I drove him.

TIBBS. Alone?

(A pause.
ENDICOTT *stiffens slightly.)*

ENDICOTT. That's right. As soon as we left, the ladies retired.

TIBBS. What time'd you get back here?

ENDICOTT. Can't give exact times.

TIBBS. You can try.

ENDICOTT. We were absorbed in other matters.

TIBBS. Where'd you drop him?

ENDICOTT. At his hotel.

TIBBS. Why didn't he stay here?

ENDICOTT. We offered but he declined.

TIBBS. Why?

ENDICOTT. We have a guest room, but his daughter was there. He chose to stay at the hotel, despite the fact it's decidedly second rate.

TIBBS. From the time you left together, did you meet anyone or see anyone until you returned?

ENDICOTT. Mr. Tibbs, I'm not sure I like the tone of that question. Are you asking me to prove an alibi? Are you suggesting I killed a very close friend and business partner?

TIBBS. I'm after information. Pure and simple.

ENDICOTT. I suggest you watch yourself.

TIBBS. Did you think championing my presence here would change how this investigation was conducted?

ENDICOTT. Certainly not!

(**MELANIE** *enters.*)

MELANIE. Are you making progress, Detective?

TIBBS. Hard to say.

MELANIE. Any indication when an arrest'll be made?

TIBBS. There's been one.

MELANIE. Oh my god...

ENDICOTT. Jesus, why didn't you say so!?

TIBBS. Because they have the wrong man.

MELANIE. Who?

TIBBS. Officer Wood.

MELANIE. The one so nice to me the day...

TIBBS. That's right.

MELANIE. He's accused...of killing my father?

TIBBS. That and more. (*to* **ENDICOTT**) Now, my question...

ENDICOTT. From the time we left here, Mr. Tibbs, I saw no one and don't believe Mr. Tatum did either. That is, up until the time I left him at the door of his motel. Then I wished him good night and came back here. There is no one, to my knowledge, who can prove what I say, but that's what happened.

TIBBS. I'm gonna ask you a few more questions and I want you be particularly careful with the answers.

(pause)

ENDICOTT. Very well...

TIBBS. I've been told Mr. Tatum often carried large sums of money. Do you know if he was doing so the last time you saw him?

ENDICOTT. Sometimes he'd have several hundred dollars on his person, but nothing beyond that. I don't consider that a large sum, but I suppose others might.

TIBBS. Was he impulsive?

(MELANIE speaks up unexpectedly –)

MELANIE. Yes. He'd make up his mind on the spur of the minute. And he was usually right when he did. If you mean, did he have a bad temper? The answer to that is "no."

TIBBS. Was you father the sort who'd make friends easily?

MELANIE. Everyone liked him.

ENDICOTT. Most...

MELANIE. Yes, most...of course.

TIBBS. One last question: Would your father have liked me?

ENDICOTT. What kind of damn question is that, Tibbs?

TIBBS. I'd like to know.

MELANIE. I'm sure of it. I've never known anyone so free of prejudice.

TIBBS. Thank you. Whether you realize it or not, you've been a great help. In a little while, I believe you'll know why.

(Lights shift to:)

Scene Twenty-nine

(The Purdy Home. **TIBBS** *knocks.* **NOREEN** *opens the door, sees* **TIBBS**.)

NOREEN. Niggers go the back door.

*(***TIBBS*** *walks past her.)*

TIBBS. This one don't.

NOREEN. Don't you come in the door!

TIBBS. Where's your father?

*(***PURDY*** *enters.)*

PURDY. Get outta here!

TIBBS. I'm from police headquarters...

PURDY. We don't want you around.

TIBBS. – Come to talk to you...

PURDY. I know who you are.

TIBBS. This is about your daughter –

PURDY. Get outta here fast or I'll break you.

TIBBS. Shut up and sit down.

PURDY. This is my house, boy!

TIBBS. I'm here about the charges you filed.

PURDY. Ain't got nothin' to talk to a black boy about!

*(***PURDY*** *grabs his shotgun from the corner.)*

And no black boy's gonna sit in my front parlor unless he's fixin' on sweepin' it. So you best pick up a broom or leave.

(Aims his shotgun at **TIBBS**.)

TIBBS. Wanna stay outta prison?

NOREEN. Pa, make 'im go away!

TIBBS. I'll go when I'm good and ready and not a second before.

PURDY. I can put you down like a sick dog, nobody'd blink.

*(***TIBBS*** *ignores the gun aimed right at him. He sits down on the couch, talks to* **PURDY** *as if invited.)*

TIBBS. You and your daughter told us somebody did her wrong. Now it's our job to see she's taken care of, and the man is punished.

PURDY. *(still pointing gun)* Sam Wood done her wrong!

TIBBS. You know Mr. Wood's been on the force for years.

PURDY. *(still pointing the gun)* And he's in jail for murder ain't he?!

(Over the following, PURDY slowly lowers his gun and eventually puts it aside.)

TIBBS. And there's reasons for that you don't know. Now about your daughter…whenever this happens and the man admits his responsibility, that's all there is to it. But Wood is stubborn. He won't admit he did it. So now all the tests have to be given.

(beat)

That is unless you can help me prove him guilty…

NOREEN. You mean I gotta tell it again?

PURDY. What tests?

TIBBS. It's hard for a man to prove he didn't have relations with a girl. Only way is through certain procedures and evidence.

NOREEN. Dad??

PURDY. Ain't no test to tell who done the dirty business with a girl.

TIBBS. There are for who didn't do it. Those are the ones you're gonna have to take.

PURDY. Like what, goddammit?

TIBBS. First, a sample of her blood. Fill up some test tubes.

NOREEN. Don't like needles stuck all in me.

PURDY. Who's gonna do that?

TIBBS. Doctors. Nobody else will touch your daughter.

PURDY. Better goddamn not.

TIBBS. Then, after, they do an examination to make sure she was violated as she says. Also, they have to find out whether or not she's going to have a baby.

(**PURDY** *leaps to his feet, grabs his shotgun again.*)

PURDY. Ain't nobody gonna look at her secrets! I'll shoot the man tries! You get outta here!

TIBBS. You wanna know these things before they come and do 'em when you're away, don't you?

PURDY. Nobody's gonna look at her secrets.

TIBBS. Only thing'll save her is if the man confesses. He says he's innocent. You filed charges...the doctor has to examine her. No other way this's gonna happen.

PURDY. Gillespie can stop it.

TIBBS. The law won't let him.

PURDY. You'll see.

TIBBS. Wood can get a court order and you'll have no choice.

PURDY. Boy, you're just full'a lies. I don't think you know half'a what you think you do.

TIBBS. I don't wanna see an innocent man framed and put in trouble. Even if it's you.

PURDY. They can't do nothin' to me. I didn't do it.

TIBBS. Suppose you get up in court and say Sam Wood is the man who got her into trouble –

PURDY. – That's exactly what I'm gonna do!

TIBBS. – Then suppose the doctor makes a mistake and says he isn't. That leaves you guilty of perjury.

PURDY. Perjury?

TIBBS. Lying. For that you go to prison.

NOREEN. Doctors don't make mistakes like that.

TIBBS. Sometimes they do, and juries believe 'em. Now suppose you tell me just how it happened, then I'll try to get Sam Wood to confess.

PURDY. Then they'll leave us alone?

TIBBS. That's right.

(*pause*)

PURDY. Tell 'im.

NOREEN. Which thing am I s'posed to say?

PURDY. Tell 'im what happened.

NOREEN. Which story?

PURDY. The way it happened.

(*pause*)

NOREEN. Well, he's always comin' past here at night all hot an' bothered, peekin' in the windows. I should of told my pa, but I was kinda scared, him being a cop and all that. Then one night, when Pa was out, he came by and knocked on the door. Said he was on his way to work. Was askin' for names of girls who would like to be queen of the music festival.

TIBBS. What music festival?

NOREEN. Just something they have by the lake every year. Said I was real cute and he wanted to put my name down for queen...

TIBBS. Go on...

NOREEN. ...Well, he sweet-talked quite a bit and said even though he worked nights, he still saw a lot of people and could get me enough votes so's I'd win. Iffin' I did, I'd win me a trip to New York. I don't remember too much after that. He gave me a drink, said he wouldn't hurt me, but would make me feel good. He said I was the future queen and everybody would wish they was me. He said in New York I'd learn to sing and dance and maybe even be in the movies. He said he could make it all come true and I oughta be real grateful to him...After that I don't remember so much except when he went away he said for me not to worry 'cause he'd been careful.

TIBBS. You're sure it was Sam?

NOREEN. It was Sam. Ain't no doubt about it.

(*Lights shift to:*)

Scene Thirty

(The jail. TIBBS *and* SAM*)*

SAM WOOD. Why don't you give up and go home.

TIBBS. Maybe this town's growing on me.

SAM WOOD. Thought you were smart.

TIBBS. Apparently not.

SAM WOOD. Well good luck.

TIBBS. I need to clear up a point or two.

SAM WOOD. It don't matter.

TIBBS. The night we rode together you changed your route.

SAM WOOD. Virgil, don't mess with this.

TIBBS. You wanted to avoid the Purdy house, right?

SAM WOOD. Have you driven past there?

TIBBS. Didn't have to. Harvey Oberst told me all I need to know.

SAM WOOD. Why you so sure I changed my route?

TIBBS. You took a short stretch of dirt road.

SAM WOOD. So?

TIBBS. When we stopped at the diner, dust was on the car.

SAM WOOD. They don't have dust in Pasadena?

TIBBS. The night you picked me up at the station there wasn't any on your car.

SAM WOOD. Maybe you didn't notice.

TIBBS. And what it means to me is you didn't go down that dirt road the night you arrested me.

SAM WOOD. Maybe I washed the car.

TIBBS. I checked the logs.

(A long pause as SAM *digests this…)*

SAM WOOD. So far, you're right.

TIBBS. Wish you'd told me this sooner. Would've saved me a lot of time.

SAM WOOD. Lots a' things I should've done different.

TIBBS. Had a talk with Purdy and Noreen. Scared 'em pretty well. Told them she'd have to be examined.

SAM WOOD. And?

TIBBS. They'll be in this afternoon. If I can get her to change her story in front of witnesses, your charges go out the window.

(Lights shift to:)

Scene Thirty-one

(*The Police Station.* **GILLESPIE** *and* **TIBBS**.
SAM *sits in the corner, hands manacled.*
PURDY *and* **NOREEN** *stand there, having just entered.*)

GILLESPIE. We have a big routine to put both of you through. The medical part of it may take some time. Is there anything you'd like to tell me before we get started?

PURDY. Noreen does. She got to chewin' over what she said and –

NOREEN. Maybe I made a mistake.

GILLESPIE. You told us about that last time.

NOREEN. I mean I guess maybe…maybe it wasn't him.

GILLESPIE. Mr. Wood?

NOREEN. Yeah.

PURDY. Noreen don't sleep so good at night some times. She seen the police car come past and she knew who was in it. Then when she went to sleep after that she dreamed about him and that's just what give her the idea

GILLESPIE. I find it hard to believe a girl like Noreen would dream so vividly about a thing that she'd come down and file a formal complaint. If she'd been a few months younger she could've put a man in danger of his life.

PURDY. Well, she ain't. She's old enough to do as she pleases.

NOREEN. Now I don't have to be examined, huh?

GILLESPIE. If you and your father state here before witnesses that the charges you placed against Mr. Wood were in error, then there's no need for a physical examination.

TIBBS. You showed courage coming here this evening. Lots of girls wouldn't have been willing to do it.

NOREEN. Pa made me.

TIBBS. There's something you can do to help. It's more important than you might think. Could you tell us how you happened to dream about Mr. Wood?

NOREEN. Well, he's a real OK guy. Never got t'meet him, but I heard talk. He's got a real good job, steady, and a car, and I just thought about 'im. Thought maybe he'd like me, especially, cause I heard he didn't have no girl.

GILLESPIE. Since you both came forward, as far as my department is concerned, we'll call it a closed incident. That doesn't mean Mr. Wood won't sue you for defamation of character; I imagine he probably will.

SAM WOOD. I don't wanna sue anybody.

PURDY. Come on, girl. We're gettin' outta here.

(NOREEN *turns to* SAM *on the way out.*)

NOREEN. I'm real sorry. Maybe some time we could get a soda together?

SAM WOOD. I don't think so.

PURDY. C'mon!

(PURDY *and* NOREEN *exit.*)

TIBBS. Any other point you want settled before you release Sam?

GILLESPIE. How you got your hands on six hundred dollars to pay off your mortgage.

TIBBS. The bank told you he had that amount, but they didn't tell you what kind of cash.

GILLESPIE. Cash is cash, don't bullshit me.

SAM WOOD. I was hoarding coins, Chief. Quarters, halves, nickels and dimes. Some bills, largest just five dollars. Tried to make it fifty cents a day.

TIBBS. You did better than that. Four dollars a week.

(*beat*)

Is he a free man now?

GILLESPIE. I s'pose he is.

TIBBS. Then I'd like you to restore him to duty so he can make his regular patrol tonight.

SAM WOOD. If it's all the same, I'd like to spend a night at home.

TIBBS. It's important you drive tonight. And I'm coming with you.

GILLESPIE. What's this about Virgil? Let the poor son of a gun get a rest.

TIBBS. There'll be plenty of time for sleep when we catch our man.

GILLESPIE. Why you so hot and bothered to get out there tonight?

TIBBS. Because unless something radical happens, before morning, Mr. Wood will arrest the murderer of Charles Tatum.

Scene Thirty-two

(**TIBBS** *rides shotgun as* **SAM** *drives.*)

SAM WOOD. Maybe we'd better check on the Endicotts, see everything's all right?

TIBBS. Go if you like, but there's better reason to stay down here.

SAM WOOD. Gonna tell me about it?

TIBBS. Rather not.

SAM WOOD. If I'm the one s'posed to arrest the guy – ?

TIBBS. Can't have you betray something at the wrong time.

SAM WOOD. Don't like the sound of that.

TIBBS. Keeping something to yourself as though you didn't have the knowledge is hard to do. Until the time comes, the fewer who know the better.

SAM WOOD. Why can't we do something about it now?

TIBBS. Would you trust me? I promise you'll be there when it goes down.

SAM WOOD. Fine.

(*long pause*)

Odd feeling this time of night. Always notice it.

TIBBS. It's a miasma in the air.

SAM WOOD. A who?

TIBBS. Certain feeling, a kind of atmosphere.

SAM WOOD. That's what I meant.

(*driving*)

Usually stop about now for my break.

TIBBS. Okay with me.

SAM WOOD. Want me to get you food?

TIBBS. No. If I think of something, I'll let you know.

(*Transition light/sound, the gravel under the car tires as they slow....to a stop.*)

Scene Thirty-three

(The diner. **RALPH** *behind the counter. Two* **BARFLIES**
drinking coffee.
SAM *enters.)*

RALPH. What'll it be, Sam?

SAM WOOD. Still thinking. And it's Mr. Wood.

*(***RALPH** *smiles to himself.* **SAM** *sits.)*

Root beer float, some toast, and a batch 'a onion rings.

RALPH. It's your stomach.

*(***TIBBS** *enters.* **RALPH** *sees this.)*

Hey, you there! Out!

TIBBS. Just want a glass of milk.

RALPH. You can't come in here. Go back outside. When
these gentlemen get through, maybe one of 'em'll
bring a carton out to you.

SAM WOOD. No problem, Ralph. I'll do it, Virgil.

TIBBS. I'm a police officer just like this man. All I want is to
sit and have something like the others.

SAM WOOD. Virgil, come on…

RALPH. I don't wanna get rough, but if my boss hears I let a
nigger in, I'll be fired. Now get outta this diner.

TIBBS. Why?

RALPH. 'Cause I told you.

*(***RALPH** *puts his hands on* **TIBBS** *' shoulders to shove
him towards the door, but –*
TIBBS *whirls on the balls of his feet, seizes* **RALPH** *'s arm
with both hands and pulls it back in a painful hammer-
lock.*
SAM *jumps to his feet.)*

SAM WOOD. Virgil! Let him go!

RALPH. Hey! Get your goddamn hands off 'a me!

(The two **BARFLIES** *jump to their feet –)*

SAM WOOD. It ain't his fault, Virgil, now stop it –

TIBBS. Sam! Arrest this man for the murder of Charles Tatum –

SAM WOOD. What??

(The **BARFLIES** *grab* **TIBBS** *from behind. They struggle.)*

Son of a bitch! Everyone hold on!

(The **BARFLIES,** **TIBBS** *and* **RALPH** *tumble into a wild brawl –*

SAM *pulls* **BARFLY #1** *off* **TIBBS,** *but* **BARFLY #1** *slugs* **SAM.***)*

BARFLY #1. Nigger-lover!

*(***SAM** *and* **BARFLY #1** *fight as –*

TIBBS *bashes* **RALPH***'s face into the counter as –*

BARFLY #2 *gets* **TIBBS** *in a headlock and they tumble into a crazy fight as –*

RALPH*, bloody, sees* **SAM** *on top of his foe, dives on* **SAM,** *not to fight, but to pull Sam's gun from this holster and then –*

TIBBS *elbows* **BARFLY #2** *in the face, then leaps on* **RALPH***. They struggle for the gun.*

BARFLY #2 *dives out the door and runs off.*

BARFLY #1 *sees his buddy fleeing and does the same.*

SAM *piles on* **TIBBS** *and* **RALPH** *as they all struggle for the gun –*

It goes off ONCE! TWICE!

TIBBS *slams* **RALPH***'s hand against the ground until he drops the gun then delivers a decisive punch that takes the fight out of Ralph.*

SAM *grabs* **RALPH** *and throws him into a chair as* **TIBBS** *gets up.*

SAM *cuffs* **RALPH***'s hands to the chair.*

Everyone panting, recovering from the brawl.)

RALPH. …You boys don't know what you're doing! You ain't got no clue!

TIBBS. I know you're under arrest for the Tatum murder.

RALPH. Nothing! You got nothing, boy! You come in here and attack me! I got witnesses –

TIBBS. I know you needed money for an abortion...and cause it was a hot night...you hit pay dirt.

RALPH. Fuck you...

SAM WOOD. You want another pop in the face, Ralph? Swear to god, I'll knock your teeth out.

RALPH. You don't know nothin'!

VIRGIL. Saw Tatum walking. Offered him a ride. Tatum told you about the demolition. You told him you wanted to see the old buildings before they came down, or some such story...

(Light Change: **TATUM** *shows* **RALPH** *the inside of one of the old buildings.)*

You found a piece of piping in the debris left inside...

TATUM. ...once we knock this down, we're gonna reinvent this section of town. Movie theater. Woolworth's Department store...you know what kind of commerce that's gonna bring in here...?

*(***RALPH*** *moves up behind* **TATUM** *and bashes him across the head!)*

RALPH. I'm sorry, mister...I just need a bit a your dough, okay? Ain't 'nothin' personal...just gonna have a little headache, that's all...

*(***RALPH*** *takes the wallet and starts to move away.*
TATUM *doesn't move.*
RALPH *looks back...*
Thinks a moment...
Goes back to the body...tries to wake him.)

Mister...hey...hey...

(The pipe drops from his hands...
Lights shift to normal:)

Bullshit...no...

TIBBS. But when you realized what you'd done...you dumped him and left him in the street.

RALPH. You way off, boy.

TIBBS. No, I'm not. And more important, I can prove it. I can prove you did it.

(A long pause as RALPH *absorbs everything that's going down. He starts to crack.)*

RALPH. Fuck! Jesus, I just didn't wanna go to jail for knocking up a piece a' jailbait! That's it!

*(*RALPH *lowers his head, shaking, breaking down.)*

Someone put a curse on me, man. I'm cursed. Got the Devil spittin' at me. He's spittin' at me!

*(*TIBBS *and* SAM *share a look: Something else is going on here.)*

TIBBS. She's not jailbait, Ralph.

RALPH. What?

TIBBS. Noreen. She's eighteen.

RALPH. She's sixteen.

SAM WOOD. No, Ralph. She ain't.

RALPH. Why you sayin' this shit to me?

SAM WOOD. It's true. Her father passed her off on account she fell behind in school.

*(*RALPH *stares, absorbing this a moment. Finally:)*

RALPH. I'm screwed anyway….It don't matter I didn't kill him no how…it don't matter cause I'm cursed.

SAM WOOD. If you didn't, who did?

RALPH. I'm dead. He can get to me.

TIBBS. Who? Who can get to you?

SAM WOOD. Nobody's gonna be gettin' to you, Ralph. Talk to us.

*(*PETE *enters.)*

PETE. Sam! The hell's going on? Comin' in for my dinner and I hear gunshots!

SAM WOOD. Call Gillespie.

(PETE *sees Sam's gun on the floor. Picks it up.*)

PETE. What's happening?

TIBBS. We got our murderer.

PETE. No, shit…

> (RALPH *has frozen…eyes the gun* PETE *is "casually" holding, but is also pointing at* RALPH.)

SAM WOOD. I'll take my gun.

PETE. What's he saying?

RALPH. *(to PETE)* You know what I'm saying.

PETE. Did he confess?

SAM WOOD. My gun…?

RALPH. I ain't doing this, Pete. Fuck you.

TIBBS. Doing what?

RALPH. I ain't takin' the rap. I don't got to.

SAM WOOD. *(attention pulled to* RALPH*)* What're you talking about?

> (TIBBS *is staring at* PETE.)

TIBBS. Sam, get your gun.

RALPH. *(now clearly to* PETE*)* You gonna shoot me in front of two cops? Huh?

SAM WOOD. Give me the gun goddammit!

> (SAM *reaches for the gun,* PETE *backs up, aiming at* SAM. PETE *pulls his own revolver to cover* TIBBS. RALPH *loses it:*)

RALPH. HE DONE IT! PETE DONE IT! I DIDN'T DO SHIT! PETE KILLED TATUM! I WAS SCARED, I SAW WHAT HAPPENED! I DIDN'T DO IT!

PETE. Naw, naw, you did it all right, and when Sam and the nigger tried to take you down you shot 'im with Sam's gun…then I shot you, you dumb son-of-a-bitch…

SAM WOOD. Don't do this, Pete. We'll clear this up…Don't do this. We can settle this, whatever happened…

> *(BAM!* PETE *shoots* SAM *with his own gun.* SAM *flounders back and doesn't move.*

RALPH's freaking out, trying to break free from the cuffs.
Impossible, obviously, but he's in pure panic.
Now both guns on **TIBBS**.)

PETE. You must think you're better'n me…

TIBBS. Why'd you kill Tatum?

PETE. Shit, you'll do your job right to the end, won't ya?

TIBBS. Why?

PETE. Like this town needs some big shots trying to fix everything and bringing in niggers to do the fixing?

TIBBS. Jobs for white men, too. Probably most of 'em.

PETE. Don't matter how many niggers get hired. Don't matter if it's five. Don't matter if it's just one. Hundred's will come lookin' for jobs. And when they come lookin' and don't find nothin', they'll stay anyway.

(Siren in the distance.)

RALPH. Do something!

*(***PETE*** shoots* **RALPH**, *blowing him backwards in his chair –*
TIBBS *dives for* **RALPH**.
PETE *fires a round as* **TIBBS** *lands on him.*
They struggle.
TIBBS *knocks the gun away –*
PETE *moves to dive after the gun, but* **TIBBS** *grabs him and takes him down hard.*
TIBBS *now on top of* **PETE** *–)*

TIBBS. Know how easy it'd be to snap your neck right now?

PETE. Fuck you!

TIBBS. Just a twitch and SNAP!

PETE. You'd like that wouldn't ya!

TIBBS. *(loud, in his ear, like he's out of control)* I WOULD LOVE IT! I WOULD LOVE TO HEAR THE SOUND OF YOUR NECK SNAPPIN'…
(Beat…is he gonna do it? Then –
CLICK!
TIBBS *snaps cuffs on* **PETE**.)

TIBBS. *(cont.)* *(a moment, Tibbs' voice is shaky, calming down)* But here's something that sounds even better: You are under arrest for the murder of Charles Tatum.

*(***TIBBS*** *gets off* **PETE,** *rushes to* **SAM.***)*

Hold on, Sam...just hold on...help's coming.

*(Sirens louder as lights fill the stage...
Fade to black.)*

Scene Thirty-four

(Police Station. Late.
TIBBS *sits, eyes shut, resting on a bench.*
A door slams open. A tired, but emotional **GILLESPIE**
storms out. Maybe he's pacing…either way, he yanks out
a cigarette and lights up.)

GILLESPIE. I don't know, Tibbs…I just do not fucking know…

TIBBS. What's that…

GILLESPIE. None of this. Pete…? My own guy? This don't make a shit load of sense to me.

TIBBS. Not your fault, if that's…

GILLESPIE. HEY! *(points to the room he just exited)* It's my own guy! Right here! Right here, next to me, the entire time! And I didn't see it!

*(***GILLESPIE*** is yelling. He's in a rage, but it's not clear if he's venting at* **TIBBS** *or himself.)*

TIBBS. Look, Chief…

GILLESPIE. Shit, you must be laughing inside…And you know what? I wouldn't blame you one bit.

TIBBS. Can I say something here?

*(***GILLESPIE*** gestures, "go ahead.")*

You throw a rock in this town, you hit someone with the exact same storm brewing inside that Pete has. That's why, you do what I do, you can't trust yourself. Not completely. Gotta keep a clear eye on the evidence and a sharp eye on your own bullshit.

(Beat. **GILLESPIE** *just staring at* **TIBBS**. *Seems like he's about to start yelling again…instead he just chuckles at that.*

GILLESPIE. That's what you do? You keep an eye on your bullshit?

TIBBS. Yep.

GILLESPIE. Seems like you spent most of your time keepin' an eye on mine.

TIBBS. A little bit of that, too.

*(Another smirk from **GILLESPIE**.)*

Sad truth is, most crimes only get solved when the bad guy messes up so badly it drops in your lap. Takes a lot of faith to do this. Gotta believe there's a higher reason for crawling through the muck looking for answers.

GILLESPIE. Maybe so...

*(**GILLESPIE** nods. A beat.)*

Hospital says Sam's gonna be out tomorrow morning.

TIBBS. He'd make a good Sergeant.

GILLESPIE. You tryin' to run my department, Virgil?

TIBBS. Just thinking if you did, Sam'd be grateful. Under those circumstances, he might forget the inconvenience he went through. Pardon me bringing it up.

*(**GILLESPIE** says nothing for a long moment.)*

GILLESPIE. How long you think it was Ralph?

TIBBS. Not until yesterday. Before that I thought it was Kaufman. So like I said, don't feel bad. Solving the crime is just as messy as the crime scene.

GILLESPIE. I'm going to write a letter to Chief Morris thanking him for your service. You did a good job.

TIBBS. Thank you.

GILLESPIE. C'mon, I'll take you to the station.

Scene Thirty-five

(The Train Station. The area is marked with a sign that says 'White.'
TIBBS *and* **GILLESPIE** *enter.* **GILLESPIE** *carries Tibbs' suitcase.)*

TIBBS. You think it'd be alright if I sat out here? It's a nice night.

(pause)

GILLESPIE. Don't think it'd make any difference. Anybody says anything, tell 'em I told you it was okay.

TIBBS. All right.

GILLESPIE. Take care of yourself. You're a credit to your race.

TIBBS. I feel the same about you.

*(***GILLESPIE*** chuckles.)*

GILLESPIE. I'm sure you do.

*(***TIBBS*** extends his hand…*

Beat. They look at each other.

GILLESPIE *exits without shaking.*
But before he's gone:)

Take care of yourself, Tibbs.

*(***TIBBS*** watches him leave. Then, when he's gone, he takes a seat on the bench.*
And waits for his train.
Lights slowly fade.)

The End

11/19

9 780573 698927